THE *FIRST* DO-IT-YOURSELF BACKGAMMON BOOK!

Ready for some backgammon? All you need is this book and a board! You don't even have to have an opponent to replay the many live games and solve the specialized situations discussed here in detail. After all, you don't want to just read about backgammon but to play it—and play it well. WINNING BACKGAMMON was written to bridge the gap between reading and actual experience, to get you started playing the game. And you will!

Michael Lawrence, who is a member of the U.S. Aces, a world-championship-winning bridge team, teaches both bridge and backgammon. This book is a skillful synthesis of his experience in playing backgammon and teaching it to others. For those entirely new to it, there is a general discussion of the game. Then there is the play section, a number of games between two players, who range in ability from fair to excellent. You will have a chance to play against both of them, to understand why each move was made! You'll learn by doing, then you can dazzle your live opponents with plays that might take others years to learn.

Here it is—the mechanics of the game, the opening plays, early objectives, doubling and redoubling, and a thorough analysis of the middle and end games. For the first time ever, the strategies of the winning game are accessible to both the beginner and the frustrated loser.

WINNING BACKGAMMON
by Michael S. Lawrence

PINNACLE BOOKS • LOS ANGELES

WINNING BACKGAMMON

Copyright © 1973 by Michael S. Lawrence

All rights reserved, including the right to reproduce this book or portions thereof in any form.

An original Pinnacle Books edition, published for the first time anywhere.

ISBN: 0-523-00860-0

First printing, November 1973
Second printing, May 1976
Third printing, December 1977

Photo by Robert Grumbles

Cover backgammon set available at Lederer de Paris, 613 Madison Avenue at 58th Street, New York, New York 10022.

Printed in the United States of America

PINNACLE BOOKS, INC.
One Century Plaza
2029 Century Park East
Los Angeles, California 90067

CONTENTS

INTRODUCTION

Welcome to the wonderful world of backgammon. If you are already a backgammon player, you don't need to be told the fascinations of the game. I know that for me and many others it was love at first sight. For years I wondered what those funny diagrams were on the back of the folding chess board. Then one day—or, in fact, evening—at an all-night party, I was introduced to the game on the reverse side of that chess board. I remember it quite well. After watching and asking questions for an hour or so, I decided I could play. Well, I did, sort of. By the time the sun came stealing in to remind us of the hour, I had managed to lose most of the games, a few dollars, and not a little pride. This, of course, would never do, and it became clear that the game would have to be learned properly. Unfortunately, as with most games, it must be learned by doing rather than by reading. We can read about a game, but until we actually play, we can't really become involved. So far, however, reader participation has been missing from backgammon publications, and I hope to correct this situation.

The material in this book consists of games with real backgammon situations. You are faced with problem after problem, decision after decision. You are the participant, not the kibitzer.

In short, you are playing backgammon as you read this book, not just reading about it.

Here is the format. There is a general discussion of backgammon for the readers who are new to the game. Then there is the play section, a number of games between two players who range in ability from fair to excellent. These games have been annotated to present some worthwhile points.

You will have a chance to play backgammon against a good-to-expert player and to see why each move was made. Or, you may see why some other move was *not* made. The important point in this book is to show the reason for making a move.

WINNING
BACKGAMMON

1

IN THE BEGINNING

Backgammon is a game of relatively few rules and easily understood objectives. Play begins with the men, or checkers, as in this diagram.

BLACK HOME

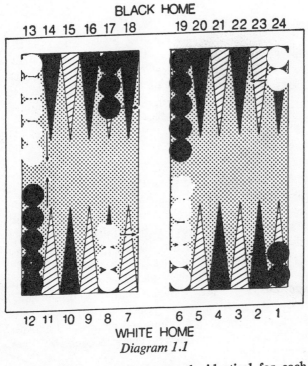

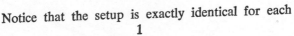

Diagram 1.1

Notice that the setup is exactly identical for each

player: the black's setup is a mirror image of the white's.

Each player will try to bring all of his men onto his home board and then to take them off the board. The player who gets all of his men off first is the winner. As indicated by the arrows in Diagram 1.1, the white men move counterclockwise, while the black men move clockwise.

Starting the Game

Each player rolls one die. The player who rolls the higher number moves first. The first roll will be the combination of the two dice. After the first move, each player rolls his own dice to determine his moves. In the event that both dice are the same, that is, doubles, the process of rolling the dice is repeated.

Moving the Men

After the dice have been thrown, the player must move the checkers in accordance with the numbers on the dice. If, for instance, he has rolled a 4–3, he must move some checker four spaces and then move another checker three spaces. Or, he may move the same checker if he wishes, moving it seven spaces.

Should he roll doubles, the same number on both dice, the player may move a total of four individual moves. This can be done by moving one checker four times, or by moving one checker three times and another once, or by moving two checkers each two times.

2

Points and Blots

If a player has two or more checkers on a point, he has what is called a *point*. This point is his, and as long as he keeps two or more checkers on it, his opponent may not land there.

In Diagram 1.2 white rolls a 6–5. Normally, white

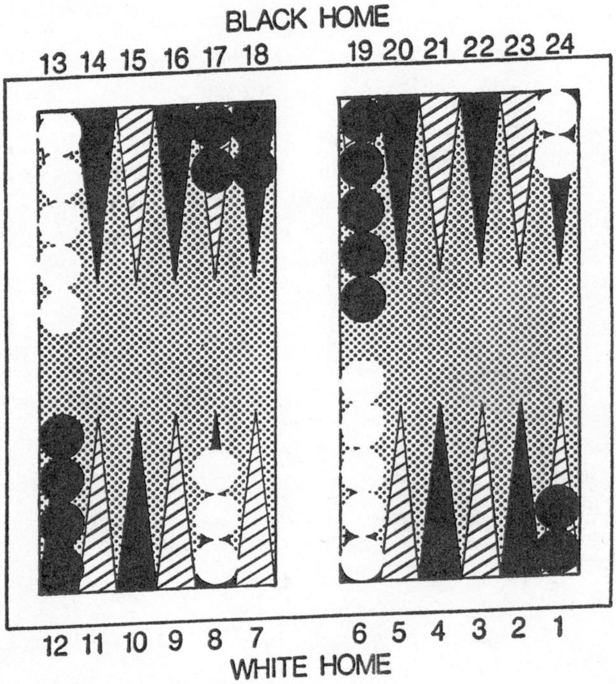

BLACK HOME

13 14 15 16 17 18   19 20 21 22 23 24

12 11 10 9 8 7   6 5 4 3 2 1

WHITE HOME

Diagram 1.2

would move a man from 24 to 13, but black's points on 18 and 19 make that play impossible.

If a player has left a man by itself, it is a *blot*. An enemy blot can be "hit" by rolling a number that lands on it. That checker now leaves the game board and must "re-enter."

Suppose white has hit a black blot. Before black can

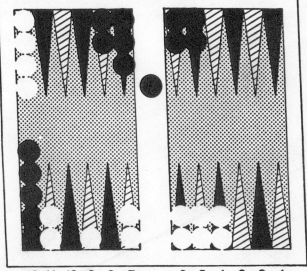

BLACK HOME

13 14 15 16 17 18   19 20 21 22 23 24

12 11 10 9 8 7   6 5 4 3 2 1

WHITE HOME

Diagram 1.3

do anything, he must get that blot back in the game. Look at Diagram 1.3. Black is on the bar (off the board), and that man must be brought back into play.

4

This is done by bringing the man onto the white home board. If black's dice include a 1, a 2 or a 3, the man on the bar can re-enter. If, however, black rolls something like 6–6 or 5–4, he cannot come in. Black will lose his complete roll, and white rolls.

If black should have two men on the bar instead of just one, as in Diagram 1.3, then he will have to get both of them in before moving his other checkers. If black rolls a 6–2, one man will re-enter on the 2, but the other cannot enter. The rest of the roll is therefore forfeited.

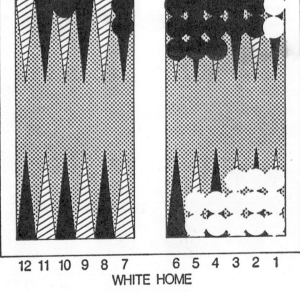

BLACK HOME

13 14 15 16 17 18   19 20 21 22 23 24

12 11 10 9 8 7   6 5 4 3 2 1

WHITE HOME

Diagram 1.4

5

There are a few other instances in which a player cannot take all or part of his move.

In Diagram 1.4, white rolls a 6–5 and has no way to play any part of it because there is no place for him to land. If in Diagram 1.4, white rolled a 6–4, the 4 could be played from point 5 to point 1, but there would be no way to play the complete roll.

Completing a Roll

If a player can possibly use a number on the dice, he must, even if it is to his detriment. Look at Diagram

BLACK HOME

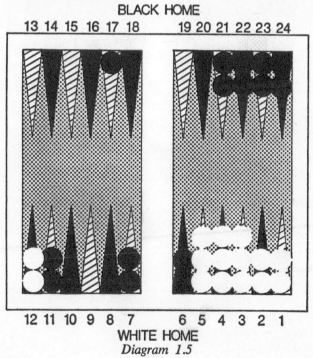

13 14 15 16 17 18   19 20 21 22 23 24

12 11 10 9 8 7   6 5 4 3 2 1

WHITE HOME
Diagram 1.5

1.5. White rolls a 6–2. It looks like white can play only the 2 and must forget the 6, but if white plays from point 12 to point 10, he can then play from point 10 to point 4. White would rather not do this, but he must play a number if he can.

BLACK HOME

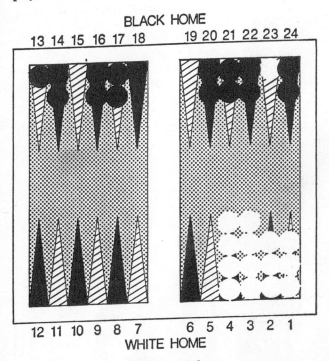

13 14 15 16 17 18   19 20 21 22 23 24

12 11 10 9 8 7   6 5 4 3 2 1
WHITE HOME

Diagram 1.6

On rare occasions, a player may find he can play the number on either die, but not both numbers. When this is the case, he must play the larger part.

In Diagram 1.6, white rolls 5–4.

7

White can move from 23 to 19 or from 23 to 18, but whichever he does, he cannot finish the roll. According to the rule, he must play the larger of the possible numbers: in this case, the 5, moving from 23 to 18.

Bearing Off

As soon as a player has all of his on his home board, he may begin to bear them off. Usually his only concern is to get his men off as quickly as possible. If he rolls a 4–2 and he has a man on the 4 point and one

BLACK HOME

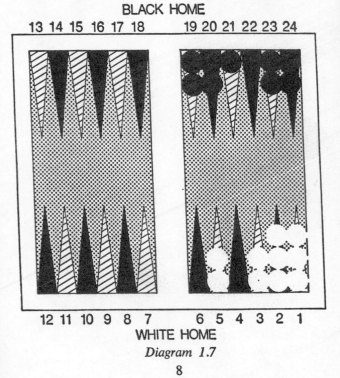

13 14 15 16 17 18   19 20 21 22 23 24

12 11 10 9 8 7   6 5 4 3 2 1

WHITE HOME

Diagram 1.7

8

on the 2 point, he simply takes one from each point and removes them from the board. These men are now out of the game. Sometimes a player will roll a number that corresponds to an empty point; that is, there is no man to take off on the corresponding point. In this case, he may do one of two things.

Look at Diagram 1.7. White has ten men left, and he rolls a 4–1. A piece can be taken off the 1 point, but there is no man on the 4 point. White instead moves a man from point 5 to point 1.

If instead of 4–1 white rolls 6–1, he takes a man off

BLACK HOME

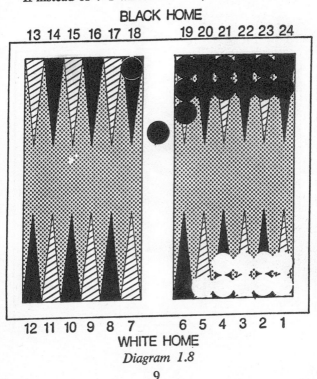

13 14 15 16 17 18   19 20 21 22 23 24

12 11 10 9 8 7   6 5 4 3 2 1

WHITE HOME

Diagram 1.8

9

the 1 point and then takes one off the 5 point. The rule is: when bearing off, if a player rolls a number that is higher than any point where there is a man on the board, he may take a man off the highest numbered point.

Sometimes, it won't be as easy as it sounds. If a player's opponent has one or more men on his board or on his bar, he may find it quite difficult to bear off safely. He may leave a blot (sometimes unavoidable), and if hit, he may lose the game. Much care must be exercised. Perhaps in the interest of safety, a player

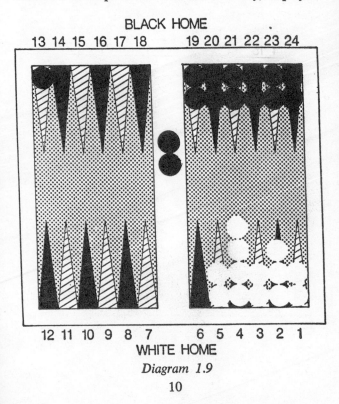

Diagram 1.9

won't take a man off for two or three rolls. Two typical examples of this kind of preventive strategy are as follows. In Diagram 1.8, white rolls a 5–1. If white takes a man off the board from the 5 point, the 1 will make a blot, regardless of how it is played. White can, however, play the 1 by moving from 5 point to 4 point, and then, according to the rule discussed earlier, he can take a man off the 4 point. This is safe and quite legal.

In Diagram 1.9, black has two men on the bar, and white rolls a 4–2. White can take a man off the 4 point and one off the 2. But if he does, he will be in the position illustrated by Diagram 1.10.

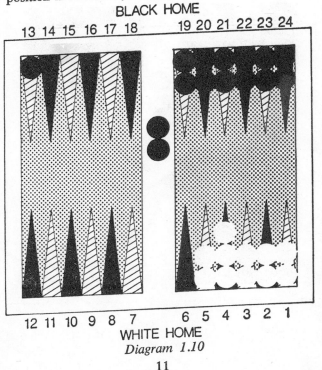

BLACK HOME

13 14 15 16 17 18   19 20 21 22 23 24

12 11 10 9 8 7   6 5 4 3 2 1

WHITE HOME

Diagram 1.10

Now white would leave a shot if he rolled 6–6, 5–5, or 4–4. If black then hit a blot, black would probably win.

In Diagram 1.9, then, white plays safe by moving both checkers on his 5 points to his 3 and 1 points. (He doesn't *have* to take men off.) This move results in the position of Diagram 1.11. Now, no number can hurt white, and if black re-enters, white will be safe since he can no longer be hit.

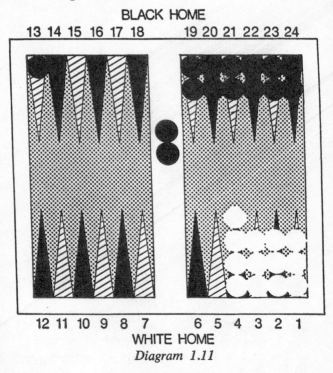

BLACK HOME

13 14 15 16 17 18   19 20 21 22 23 24

12 11 10 9 8 7   6 5 4 3 2 1

WHITE HOME

Diagram 1.11

If after bearing off one or more men, a player gets

12

hit, he will have to get those men back around the board to his home board before he can begin again to take men off.

Scoring

The player who gets all his men off first wins the game. In the event that the opponent has not been able to take a man off, the winner will be paid double. Such a situation is called a *gammon*. If, when a player has gotten all his men off, and his opponent not only has not taken a man off, but has a man on either the bar or on the winner's home board, the winner has a back-gammon, worth *triple*.

Once a player has taken a man off, he is no longer subject to being gammoned or backgammoned, regardless of what should occur.

2

OBJECTIVES AND PRIORITIES

Opening Roll

Once the game has begun, each player is going to be involved in the following endeavors:

1) Escape with his back checkers (those on point 1 or on point 24)

2) Block his opponent's back checkers.

A good place to start is with the opening roll. It is imperative to know how to play each opening number, and it is important to know why the play is made. It is white's play.

6-5   Run a back man to safety. This is known as *lover's leap.*

6-4   Run a back man to 14 point (black's 11 point). *Don't* make the 2 point. The 2 point is safe, but as the beginner will see when he starts to play, the 2 point is worthless in the early game.

6-3   Run a back man to 15 point (black's 10 point). An alternative is to play one man to black's bar point (black's 7 point) and come down to the 10 point from 13. Don't try this move until comfortable with the other recommended plays.

6-2   Run a back man out, or bring one from 13 point to 5 point. The purpose of the second play is to try to secure the 5 point. Should black not hit white's blot, white will have excellent chances to make a point on the 5 point with his next roll. Playing 6-2 in this fashion is an effort to block or contain the opponent's back men. Playing 6-2 by running is the reciprocal. This roll is a bad number, and the player must take a gamble one way or the other. I prefer the second way in an effort to contain black's back men.

6-1   This is a super roll for white to make his bar point. Now, if the opponent rolls 6-5 or 6-6, it will not be nearly as good as it would be normally because he can no longer play in the normal fashion; white has made the bar point, blocking black.

5–4 Bring two men down to white's 9 and 8 points. White hopes to roll some number on his next turn to make a point, taking advantage of the extra builder on 9.

5–3 This is close. White can make the 3 point, or he can bring two men down to the 8 and 10 points. I slightly prefer the latter. The 3 point is not very valuable this early in the game, but the alternative play increases his chances of making the 4, 5, or bar points.

5–2 Bring two men down to the 11 and 8 points, hoping the extra builder (an extra man that may hopefully be used to help build another point) on 11 will subsequently help to make an additional blocking point.

5–1 Use the 5 to go to the 8 point. Now, for the 1, white can play conservatively and split the two back men, or he can be aggressive and play from his 6 point to his 5 point.

4–3 Bring two men to 10 and 9 points, hoping to use these later to make a point.

4–2 Make the 4 point.

4–1 Just like 5–1, bring a man to point 9 and then decide between splitting the back men or slotting a man on the 5 point. I prefer to slot, but there are substantial arguments on both sides.

15

3–2 Bring two men to 11 and 10 points. Hope to make a point on the next roll.

3–1 The best of all opening rolls. Make the 5 point.

2–1 Bring a man to 11 point and then, as with 5–1 and 4–1, select either the conservative play of splitting the back men, or the one of slotting on the 5 point.

A player must know the openings. As with all things in life, if one gets off to a bad start, it is hard to recover. If the beginner learns these openings and *understands* why they are played, he will have taken a major step in learning backgammon.

Early Use of Doubles

Often a player will be treated to a set of doubles on his first roll. Assuming his opponent's first roll has not given him reason to do otherwise, he should play doubles these ways.

6–6 Make both bar points.

5–5 Bring two men down from the 13 point to the 3 point.

4–4 Either go to the 5 point by bringing two men from 13, or make black's 5 point and white's own 9 point. If black has made his bar point, white should definitely move his back men to black's 5 point to avoid being trapped.

3–3 Make the 5 and 3 points or make the bar point. However, if the opponent has made his

16

bar or his 5 point, white should use 3–3 to
make black's 4 point and his own 5 point.

2–2   Make the 4 and 11 points. However, if black
has made his bar point, white should grab
black's 5 point.

1–1   Grab the bar and 5 point.

There are reasons why a player might not make these
plays: 1) His opponent's first move has made them
impossible because he has made a blocking point. 2)
The player may decide to hit a blot instead. More on
this later.

3

THE EARLY GAME

Escaping with the Back Men

In the early game, the player will be concerned with
getting his two back men to safety. However, if his
opponent (henceforth known as black) has not made
any points on his board (in the early stages, one should
only worry about the bar, and the 5 and 4 points), he
should run only when he has nothing better to do.

The running numbers are usually 6–6, 6–5, 6–4, and
6–3. If the player can make an important point on his
board with one of these running numbers, that move
takes priority. (See *Containing*.)

If black has started to make his board, white may decide to play 3–3 and 2–2 by moving his back men up. With 2–2, he normally makes his 11 and 4 points. If black has made his bar point, white should use 2–2 to grab black's 5 point. This play guarantees that white will be able to get away later.

The reason one doesn't always play 3–3 and 2–2 in this way is that it is more important to make points in one's own board. Only when the player is in danger of being trapped does he make this play in the early stages of a game.

Splitting the Back Men

In the early part of the game, it is often wise to split the two back men. This move is usually made for one of three reasons.

1. Splitting increases the number of rolls, which allows the back men to escape. When the game starts, 6–5 is the only roll that can allow escape with complete safety. If a player moves a back man up one point to his opponent's 2 point, he can escape with 5–5 as well.

Splitting acquires its main importance when the opponent has started to make his board. If black has made his 5 point, white can no longer run with 5–4. However, if white's back men are split, on black's 1 and 2 points, 5–4 can then be used to escape, if it appears best. See Diagram 3.1.

As soon as it seems that the back men are in danger, consider splitting them in hopes of escaping.

When considering a split, try to split only to the opponent's 2 point. The reason for this is that the opponent will not be likely to hit on his 1 or 2 points.

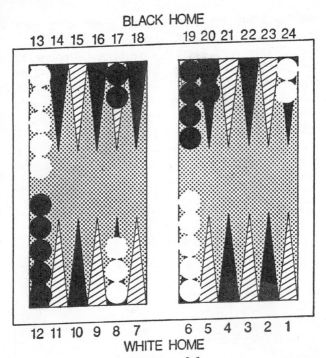

Diagram 3.1

It is usually a losing proposition for him to do so, since he must bring his men too far forward, where they become valueless. Furthermore, if the player subsequently rolls 3–2 or 4–3, he may be able to make black's 4 or 5 points with what were otherwise poor rolls.

Splitting a man to the 3, 4, or 5 points is not recommended, if it is avoidable. The opponent will be much more inclined to hit the blot. In fact, there are a large number of rolls that will enable him to both hit the blot and cover as well. In Diagram 3.2, black can and will hit white's blot with a 6, 3, or 1, plus assorted com-

19

binations. Rolls like 6–1, 3–1, 6–3, 4–4, 3–3, and 1–1 point on the blot.

2. Splitting puts pressure on the opponent's outer board. Whenever black has escaped with both of his back men (say, he rolled 6–5 twice), black should split. White is going to have to put some blots somewhere, unless he is very lucky. If he doesn't split, black will leave his blots on his outer board where they will be available to use later for making points on his inner board. By splitting white increases his chances of hitting

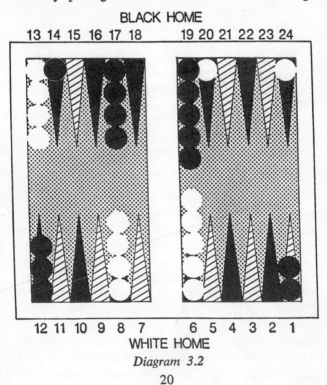

BLACK HOME

13 14 15 16 17 18   19 20 21 22 23 24

12 11 10 9 8 7   6 5 4 3 2 1

WHITE HOME

Diagram 3.2

those blots. In fact, if black has escaped with his back men in the first two rolls, it is almost mandatory that white split.

3. Another reason for splitting is that the player may not wish to take a number somewhere else on the board. It may be that a split is the least dangerous move available.

Containing

In the early part of a game, a player should be involved in making up his own board. Whenever something constructive can be done in this direction, he should do it in preference to running or splitting. Usually, numbers that are used for running have little value in building one's board, but situations like the following occur. White rolls 5–2, bringing two men to his 11 and 8 points. Black rolls 5–4, moving to his 9 and 8 points. See Diagram 3.3.

Now white rolls 6–4. He doesn't run! Instead, he makes his bar point. Notice that 6–3 would make his 5 point. A good idea, if a player starts instinctively to run, is for him to look elsewhere to see if he has something better to do.

While making up his board, a player should not worry too much about leaving blots open for his opponent. Certainly, one doesn't leave blots all over the board, but when a player can leave a blot for a constructive purpose, it may well be right to do so. Note that the opening rolls of 5–1, 4–1, and 2–1 are frequently played by slotting a man on the 5 point. Less dangerous, of course, is to bring a man to one of the outer points—9, 10 or 11—where it can be hit only

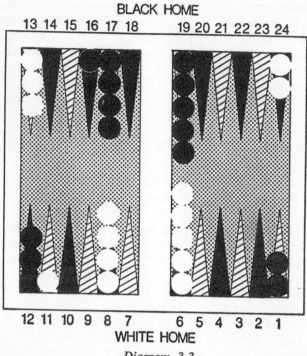

Diagram 3.3

with a combination shot. This blot can be used as a builder, and, with luck, the player may be able to use it to make an additional point. However, even though it is safer, this move is less likely to be of use than slotting.

When considering whether or not to leave a blot, the player must decide whether he minds getting hit. In the early part of the game, it is reasonably safe to slot. But as soon as the opponent has begun to build a board,

22

one must be more and more careful about leaving a shot (a blot which the opponent may be able to hit).

In general, a player should try to make additional points in this order.

1. 6 point. He starts with this point. For practical purposes, one should not release this point until bearing off.

2. 5 point. This point is the start of the inner board. Not only does it serve as a block against the opponent's back men but it allows the player to put builders there to be used in making additional inner points.

3. Bar point. This blocks 6–6 and 6–5 and turns these rolls, usually good for the opponent, into poor ones. In the first few moments of a game, the bar point may be more valuable than the 5 point.

4. 4 point. This is a useful point, but it is of primary value when the 5 point has been made as well. The problem with the 4 point by itself is that the opponent can advance to the 5 point and thus the blocking value of the 4 point is negated.

5. 3 point. Its value is slight until a player has made the 5 and/or the 4 point.

Some General Guidelines—Errors to Avoid

Usually it is a bad policy to hit a blot on the 1 or 2 points. Doing so advances a man to a position where

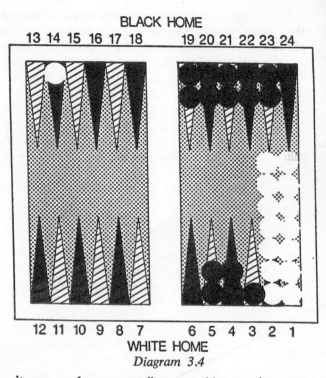

Diagram 3.4

it can no longer contribute anything to the contest. Diagram 3.4 illustrates an extreme case.

White has burned all of his men. The only possible value of those fourteen men on the 1 and 2 points is that they can be taken off quickly in the bear off. Far better for white to have those pieces spread out over a few points. Then that lone white blot might have a chance of getting home safely. As it is, white will be incredibly lucky to escape this position. Even one checker wasted on the 1 or 2 points weakens the overall position.

There is one exception to this rule of not hitting on the 1 point. If the opponent has split his back men, a player may be able to hit *both* of his opponent's checkers with only one of his. If the opponent fails to re-enter both his men, the player may have time to do something he otherwise might not have been able to do.

Incidentally, if a player does hit his opponent's checker on the 1 point, it will probably be better for him if he gets hit when his opponent re-enters the board. If white's man on the 1 point gets hit, he can relocate it to a more useful position. Otherwise, it may sit and stagnate on the 1 point for the duration of the game.

If a player finds himself with a blot on the 1 point, he shouldn't bother covering it until necessary. Covering it merely means that he will have *two* wasted men instead of just one. When the opponent tries to make either his or the other 5 point, the rule is HIT. One should not let him do it if possible. If the opponent slots a man on his 5 point on the opening roll, one's first priority is to hit it. One should not let the opponent get away with making his 5 point easily. The only roll with which a player should not hit his opponent is 1–1, which should be used to make the bar and 5 point.

4

MIDDLE OF THE GAME STRATEGY

Once the game has started and the first few moves have been made, the game will begin to take some sort of form. It will be recognized as a back game, a running game, etc.

There are too many kinds of games to warrant discussion of them individually. Instead, a few guidelines can be presented, but the rest must come from experience. Soon, however, in the play section, the reader will be able to play backgammon and to see what it's about. Many specific situations will come up, which will be discussed in their turn.

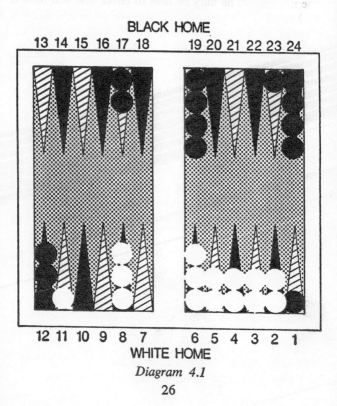

BLACK HOME

13 14 15 16 17 18   19 20 21 22 23 24

12 11 10 9 8 7   6 5 4 3 2 1

WHITE HOME

Diagram 4.1

Generalities

If a player has some of his opponent's men trapped, he should attempt to get them behind a 6-point prime (6 points in a row). The risks to be taken must be determined by the dangers of being hit. Look at Diagram 4.1.

Here, it is quite safe to slot a man on the bar. If white gets hit, he will have no trouble coming back in. Should he not get hit, he may be able to cover and will have a prime. He will almost surely win the game and likely a

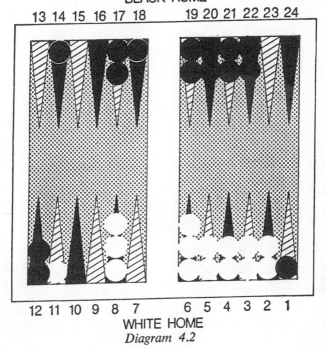

BLACK HOME

13 14 15 16 17 18   19 20 21 22 23 24

12 11 10 9 8 7   6 5 4 3 2 1

WHITE HOME

Diagram 4.2

gammon. On the other hand, in Diagram 4.2, white doesn't want to try that play. If he should be hit, he would have almost a sure loss.

Here, since he can't afford to be hit, he must play in as safe a fashion as the dice permit.

Often a player will find that his opponent has managed to escape safely with his back checkers. Should this happen, he shouldn't despair. The one thing he must not do is to stop making points on his board. Black's men may have gotten out safely, but they are not necessarily all the way home. Usually something like the positions in Diagram 4.3 occur.

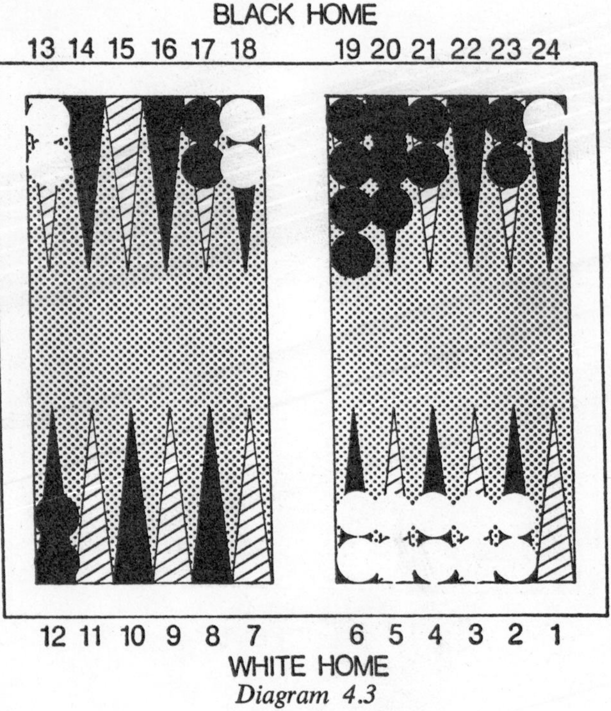

BLACK HOME

Diagram 4.3

If black rolls a 6–2, he will hesitate to bring a man from white's 12 point to his board. Doing so would give white a direct shot at his remaining man on 12, and the positions on the board are so good that he just can't afford to be hit. Probably black will bring his two men on his 8 point inside, but even though this move is momentarily safe, it may lead to problems should black roll a 6 next time. If, instead of the good board in Diagram 4.3, there is a sloppy board with few points and many blots, a board like in Diagram 4.4, then things are not so good for white.

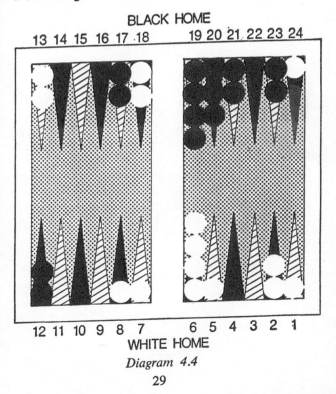

BLACK HOME

13 14 15 16 17 18   19 20 21 22 23 24

12 11 10 9 8 7   6 5 4 3 2 1

WHITE HOME

Diagram 4.4

Black can play 6–2 by bringing a man onto his board from the 12 point. White's board holds no fear for black, since it will be easy for him to come in and he may well hit a blot in the process. Black doesn't mind giving a shot when the consequences of being hit are so mild.

5

LATER DECISIONS

Sometimes it is possible to play in such a way as to guarantee no further contact between opposing men. When this happens, the situation is known as a running game, and the race goes to the player who can roll the largest numbers.

Simply speaking, a player should endeavor to get into a running game when he is ahead in pips. If he is behind in the race, he should try to maintain contact, hoping to get a shot. Look at Diagram 5.1. White rolls a 6–5. What should he do?

He should bring those two back men to his 11 and 10 points. He is quite ahead in the race, and he can determine how much he is ahead by counting the pips. Black's count is 113. This count is reached by noting the point each checker is on and adding the total of these numbers.

For instance, black has:

1 man on the 1 point	1
2 men on the 4 point	8
2 men on the 5 point	10
2 men on the 6 point	12
3 men on the 7 point	21
2 men on the 11 point	22
3 men on the 13 point	39
	113

BLACK HOME

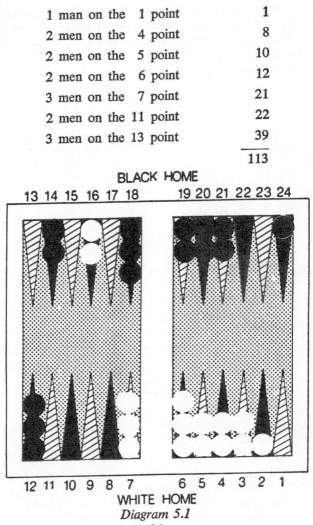

Diagram 5.1

31

Before playing the 6–5, the white men have a count of 97. White, being ahead in the count with the lowest number, should therefore turn the game into a simple race.

In Diagram 5.2, the reverse is true.

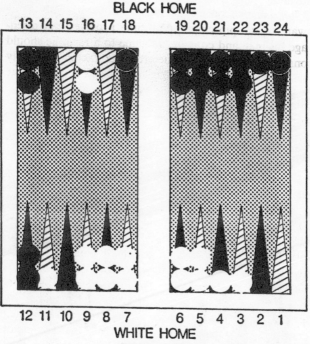

BLACK HOME
13 14 15 16 17 18   19 20 21 22 23 24

12 11 10 9 8 7   6 5 4 3 2 1
WHITE HOME
Diagram 5.2

White does not have much chance in a running game since he is 24 pips behind. Instead of taking his two men back off black's home board, he leaves them in the hope of hitting one of black's men on the 12 and 13 points.

Even if white doesn't get to hit a black man, it is

possible that black will have to waste quite a few pips. If black cannot move one of his outside men safely, he may have to move one of the men already on his board. This play does him no appreciable good, and in the meantime, white will be bringing his men in safely and advantageously.

It is very important, in later situations like this, to be aware of the pip count. Any time a player can disengage his men and commit the game to a race, he should consider doing so. The determining factor is simply "who is ahead in the race." If it's you, run! If it's your opponent, stay.

The Back Game

Every now and then things don't go as a player would like, and he finds that everytime he leaves a blot, it gets hit. Before he knows it, he has four, five, or even more men on his opponent's board.

Before the reader continues, he should ask himself this simple question: How much does it bother you to have all those men back there? Or conversely, how do you feel when you've hit a bunch of your opponent's men that are now occupying your inner board?

Strangely enough, having four or five men back on black's board does not mean the end of the world. In fact, if a player can manage to secure two, or even three, points on his opponent's board, he will have a good chance to win the game. The acquisition of these points is known as a "back game."

A good back game, properly played, will more often than not lead to a win. But, before rushing to get into back games at every available opportunity, bear this one fact in mind: Even though a player may win more games than he loses, many of the games he loses will be gammons, or even backgammons. Therefore, whenever he loses a game, he pays off at two or three to one, whereas when he wins, he gets only one point.

To answer the question of how one should feel about being hit repeatedly, he should feel that with a little luck, he will be the favorite to win the game, but he would just as soon call the whole thing off.

Prerequisites for a Back Game

In order to have a successful back game, the player must have two points on black's inner board. Having two points rather than one makes it very difficult for black to get his men on his board and then to bear them off without having a shot for white. Not only does possession of two points make it much harder for black to play safe, but when white does get the hoped-for shot, he has men on two points, all aiming at black's blot, not just men on one point. This situation almost doubles white's chances of hitting the blot when the opportunity arises.

On rare occasions, a player may be able to establish three points on his opponent's board. Now black's problem is almost insurmountable. However, this situation means that white must have at least six men back, and he has to be lucky enough to come in and make three points rather than merely coming on a point already held. Black can circumvent this situation by refusing to hit any more white men. Even if white does manage to get three points, it leaves him with only nine other men to build his board. All in all, he should not worry too much about this possibility.

Frequently, after having been hit, a player will have

options on where to play his man when re-entering the board. When this happens, he should try to make either the 1 and 3 points or the 1 and 2 points. These two combinations of points are the most effective for back games. The reason that these points are more useful than other possible combinations of two points is that they are a threat to the opponent during his entry onto his board and during his bear off. If white has some combination such as the 1 and 5 points, black may be able to get his men past white's on the 5 point and will then have only one of white's points to worry about.

BLACK HOME

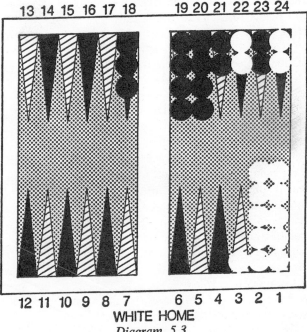

Diagram 5.3

There is another factor that is very important when considering a back game: timing. The reason for playing a back game is that a player hopes to hit his opponent's man and then to take advantage of that play.

In Diagram 5.3, white's timing is hopeless. If he hits a man, there is no way he will be able to make use of it. His men are too far advanced. Black will come in and run around the board at his convenience.

On the other hand, in Diagram 5.4, hitting a black man will give white an excellent chance to win.

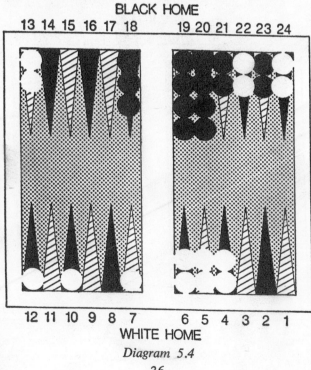

BLACK HOME

13 14 15 16 17 18   19 20 21 22 23 24

12 11 10 9 8 7   6 5 4 3 2 1

WHITE HOME

Diagram 5.4

In Diagram 5.4, white has the timing necessary for a back game. All of his men are working for him, whereas in Diagram 5.3, the opposite was the case.

Diagram 5.5 is a typical situation in which white must decide whether or not to try for a back game. What does he do with 6–6?

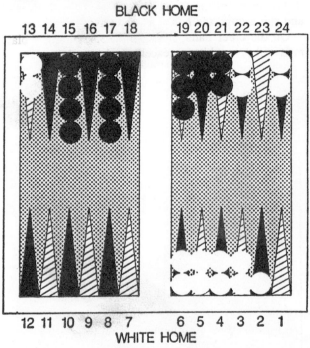

BLACK HOME

13 14 15 16 17 18   19 20 21 22 23 24

12 11 10 9 8 7   6 5 4 3 2 1

WHITE HOME

Diagram 5.5

In this position, it is right for white to give up the back game. He could keep his back points by moving both on point 13 to point 1, but he would then be too far advanced to take advantage of his back positions.

Better for him to play 24–18–12 24–18–12. This gets two men on the way home and keeps some pressure on black. Certainly, his position won't be as nice as possible, but it does give black *some* problems that the other play would not.

If, after a player has established the necessary two points for a back game, he then gets some more men sent back, he should try, when re-entering the board, to get at least one of those extra men on the forward point (that point nearest the bar point). This is necessary so that when he is later forced to leave with a checker from that front point, he won't have to leave a shot in doing so.

6

BEARING IN

When a player is bringing his checkers to his home board, in preparation for bearing them off, he should follow this general principle: don't waste pips. This means simply that he should always try to bring the men in as quickly as possible. Look at Diagram 6.1. White has rolled a 5–1.

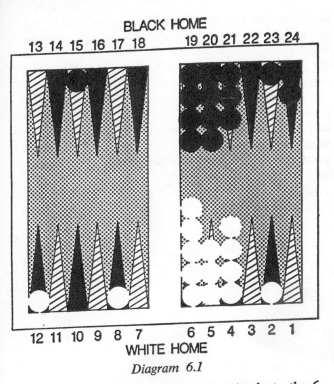

Diagram 6.1

He should bring the man on the 12 point in to the 6 point; he should not make the mistake of bringing the man on the 8 point to the 3 point just because there is no man there. If a player always brings his men to the 6, 5, or 4 points when possible, and to the 3, 2, or 1 point when necessary, he will be about as efficient as he can be.

MATHEMATICS OF BACKGAMMON

There are a number of mathematical considerations in backgammon. As a beginner plays and becomes serious about the game, these things will become more important. For the time being, however, there is only one concept that a beginner should definitely know.* He should know how to compute the chances of a blot he is leaving getting hit. Can he put the blot in a safer place, should safety be his concern?

If a player has left a blot, it can be hit by various combinations. Let's say he has a blot next to an opposing man. How often can that man hit the blot? That man will hit if the opponent rolls a 1 on either of his two dice. Here are the possible ways.

Die one: 6 5 4 3 2 1 1 1 1 1 1
Die two: 1 1 1 1 1 1 2 3 4 5 6

Notice that there are eleven possible rolls that hit the blot. Also notice that 1–1 occurs only once while 1–3 or 1–5, etc., occurs twice. Be aware that there are two ways to roll any combination that is not doubles. Therefore, one's chances to roll any *specific* number, that is, a 6, a 5, or a 1, are exactly 11/36. Thirty-six is the total number of possible combinations that one can roll.

If the blot is further away from the opponent's man,

*A complete dissertation on the theory of backgammon mathematics can be found in *The Backgammon Book* by Oswald Jacoby and John R. Crawford (Viking Press, 1970).

the odds of its being hit change. Suppose the blot is six spaces away from the opponent's man. Now it can be hit by any combination with

  6, which is 11/36 chances;
  5–1, which is 2/36 chances;
  4–2, which is 2/36 chances;
  3–3, which is 1/36 chance;
  2–2 which is 1/36 chance;
  or a total of 17/36 chances.

Look at Diagram 7.1 and determine how often the blot on point 18 can be hit.

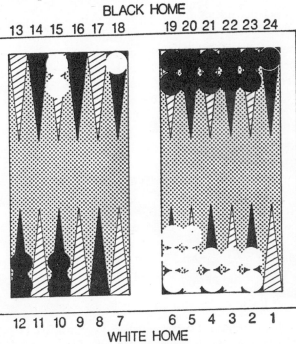

BLACK HOME

13 14 15 16 17 18 19 20 21 22 23 24

12 11 10 9 8 7 6 5 4 3 2 1

WHITE HOME

Diagram 7.1

41

The man on 12 point hits with any combination including 6, eleven possibilities; 5–1, two possibilities; 4–2, two possibilities; 2–2, one possibility; but *not* 3–3. Doubles of threes have been blocked, so there are sixteen ways instead of the usual seventeen to hit a blot six spaces away.

The man on 10 point hits the blot with these numbers: 6–2, two ways; 5–3, two ways; 4–4, one way; 2–2, one way. There are six ways for the men on 10 to hit the blot.

However, these calculations do not mean that the blot can be hit twenty-two times $(16 + 6)$. If one looks at the possible rolls that hit from both points, he will see that 6–2 and 2–2 hit from both points. But he can only count these numbers once. The *additional* numbers that hit from the 10 point are 5–3 and 4–4, or three new ways not already counted. The total, therefore, is 19 ways in which the blot can be hit.

8

PLAY SECTION

How to Use the Play Section

To get the most out of this section, the reader will need to have:

1. A backgammon set.
2. A knowledge of how the game is played. The reader need not play well (that's what this book is in-

tended to show him) but he must know the mechanics of the game. If there are any questions about the rules, refer to the previous chapter.

3. Since most backgammon is played with a doubling cube, that feature has been used throughout this text. For the time being, it might be better if the reader plays the games once without regard for the cube. Then as he begins to develop a feel for the game and has read the section on the cube, it would be a good idea for him to replay the games with the doubling cube in mind.

Here is the board setup as it will be used.

BLACK HOME

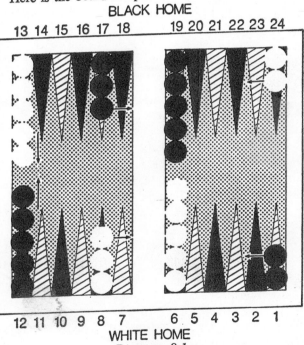

Diagram 8.1

43

Notice that the board is numbered from one to twenty-four rather than from one to twelve, on both the top and bottom. This system facilitates describing each move and acquaints the beginner with counting pips when it is necessary.

Here is how each move is described.

B   5–4
Black has rolled a 5 and a 4.

W   3–3
White has rolled double 3's.

B   4–1
Black next rolls a 4 and a 1.

The next paragraph combines the roll with the way it was played.

B   5–4   12–16   12–17
Black has rolled a 5 and a 4 and has moved one man from the 12 point to the 16 point and one man from the 12 point to the 17 point.

W   6–1   13–7   8–7
White plays his 6–1 by moving one man from the 13 point to the 7 point and one man from the 8 point to the 7 point.

B   4–3   12–16–19
Black uses his 4–3 by moving one man from the 12 point to the 16 point and on to the 19 point.

44

W 5–2 16–11X 9–7

White rolls a 5–2 and plays his 5 by moving from the 16 point to the 11 point. The X indicates that an enemy blot was hit with this move. The 2 was played by moving from the 9 point to the 7 point.

17–20

B 3–3 17–20 12–15X–18X

Black moves two men from 17 point to 20 point. One checker on 12 goes to 15, hitting a blot, and then moves on to 18, hitting another blot.

W 4–2 B–23 8–4

White had a man off the board (on the bar) and he came in from the bar with B–23 with the 2. The 4 was played by moving a checker from point 8 to point 4.

B 6–1 18–19–0

Black is bearing his checkers off the board. This roll brought the checker on point 18 to the 19 point and then off the board (0).

W 6–2 B–23 Ø

The 2 was played by bringing a checker in from the bar (B-23). The Ø indicates the other part of the roll (6) was not playable.

B 6–2 Ø

Black can play neither number. This situation usually occurs when one or more men are on the bar and they are not able to come in with the number rolled.

W 5–4 5–0 3–0

White is bearing off and takes a man off the 5 point and one man off the 3 point.

Ready for some backgammon?

You will need your board. I suggest also that you have a live opponent, but that is not necessary.

If you do play alone, I suggest you do not read the discussion on what your opponent is doing or why he is doing it. Instead, be concerned only with your men and your problems. Later, you can replay the game and look at it from the other side of the board. In this way you will get maximum benefit.

One last idea. If you number your board in the same fashion as the board is numbered in the book, it will make moving the men much easier until you have become accustomed to the game.

Finally, a backgammon game. Remember to think first before looking at the answer!

GAME 1

B	5–4	12–16	12–17

Standard. This roll is not a super, but it has its benefits. If the 16 lives (doesn't get hit), it may prove to be a useful builder.

W	1–1	6–5	8–7
		6–5	8–7

This roll is so strong that white is already a favorite.

B	3–3	1–4	17–20
		1–4	17–20

An excellent comeback roll for black. Normally black would play

17–20	19–22,
17–20	19–22,

46

but with white making his 5 and 7 points, it is wise for black to move his back men up as here. Otherwise, they might have trouble getting out later. This roll is so good for black that both players are now even again.

W   **4–2**   **13–9–7**
White leaves the 8 point alone because he hopes to make a point there on his next roll. Of course if black rolls a 4, black will hit the blot on 8. If white wanted to play conservatively, he could play 8–6–2.

B   **6–3**   **19–22**   **16–22**
Black makes his 22 (3) point.

W   **5–3**   **13–8**   **24–21**
As he has hoped, white makes the 8 point. White had 15/36 ways to accomplish this move. Any 5, 4–1, or 3–2 would do.

B   **6–2**   **12–14–20**
Black would have preferred to make a point on 21, but this roll was not too good. Notice that black did not play 4–10–12 to safety. This play would leave a blot on 4 point, which would be in grave danger. A strong alternative for black is 12–18   19–21X.

W   **6–3**   **24–18**   **21–18**
This point that white has just made is black's bar point. This was a good roll for white, because it allowed him to move up both back men safely.

B   **6-1**   **17-23**   **20–21**
This is a bad roll for black. There is no way to play

it safely. Playing as here means that white can hit with only 1's. Notice that black again refrains from running with a back man (on point 4).

W	6–2	13–11–5

B	4–3	17–21	19–22

This makes an impressive board for black, although the tempo of the game favors white. Black is advanced and is unlikely to be able to maintain a good position.

W	4–1	6–5–1

White leaves the extra man on point 7 in order to be able to play a 6 (if he rolls one) without leaving from 13 or 8 should he wish to stay.

B	5–3	4–9–12

Black moves a man to safety. This move is no bargain, but all other moves are worse.

W	1–1	7–6–5–4X
		5–4

White will double unless black gets a good roll.

B	1–1	B–1X–2–3	22–23

1–1 is even better for black than it was for white. It may even have been the only roll to save him. Notice that black played B–1–2–3 instead of 19–20–21. Black will need to escape and the former move is the way to start.

W	6–2	Ø

B		Double
W		Resign

There is no way in which white can accept this double. Even if white can come in, he is in trouble. If he stays out for a couple of rolls, he can find himself gammoned.

Games like this are quite annoying. Just when a player thinks he's winning, he meets disaster. Remember, there are as many sensational rolls for one player as for another. It is just necessary to take as much advantage of them as does the opponent.

It may seem that some of the moves that were made were not for the best. The games in this book were played by people, ranging from reasonable to expert in ability. Most of the moves were good, and some were exceptional. As with most games, however, there were a few mistakes, which have been noted in the analyses that go with the moves. On the other hand, there were some situations which were so unclear that two recognized experts would argue over what was right and what was wrong. But then, if backgammon were so clear-cut, it would hardly be the challenge it is.

GAME 2

B	5–2	12–17	12–14
W	6–3	13–7–4	

Normally a player would run with a back man, 24–18–

15, hoping to escape on the next roll. But black's man on point 14 gives him an extra chance to hit white if he makes that move. The move here gives white chances to make his 4 point if black misses him. (Black can hit white 14/36 times, any 3, 2–1, or 1–1.)

B   5–3   1–4X–9
Hit and run.

W   2–1   B–23   6–5
White shouldn't make the 23 point. It has no value at present. Instead, he should try to make his inner board points.

B   3–3   17–20   19–22
                   17–20   19–22
It is much more important for black to make two points on his board than it is for him to run with the man on point 8. This is an excellent roll.

W   5–3   13–8–5

B   2–1   9–10–12

W   5–3   8–3   6–3

The 3 point is more valuable when the 4 and/or 5 point is held as well.

B   5–4   12–16   14–19
This play keeps things reasonably safe. Black would have liked to run with the back man, but white's 5 and 6 points stopped him.

W	5–1	13–8	24–23

B	4–1	12–16	19–20

The 16 point here is automatic. Notice that one builder each on points 19 and 20 is better than two builders on 19 and none on 20.

W	6–5	24–18	23–18

White makes black's bar point. This is a good roll.

B	6–4	17–23	19–23X

Black is now in a strong position.

W	3–1	B–24	8–5

White shouldn't play B–24–21. If black rolled 4–1, 5–1, 5–5, or 5–4, he would put a point on 21, and white would be destroyed. There are also those rolls that "pick and pass," or "hit and run," such as 5–2, 4–2, and 2–1, which allow black to hit and leave a blot. As actually played, even if black does have a good roll, white may not be hit. Now white will need only a 6 to escape. Otherwise, white might find himself needing a 6 *and* a 1.

B	6–6	16–22	17–23	1–7
		16–22		

Each of these moves is forced; there were no alternatives. 6–6 was not such a good roll for black. If white hits the 7 blot, he will probably win the game.

W	6–4	13–7X	13–9

B	4–1	B–4	23–24X

Black must hit in order to gain time. If not, white would be able to devote all of his next roll to putting a point on black's blot on point 4.

W   **4–2**   **B–21**   **9–7**

White comes in and is able to get rid of both his blots on points 9 and 7. Lucky. If black had not hit on the previous move, white could have played the 4–2 to make a point on 4.

B   **6–5**   **4–10**   **19–24**

This is a poor roll. White can hit black with any 2, 5–3, 4–4, or 6–5, making 16/36 chances. Playing 4–10–15 would leave 27/36 chances. (Try working them out.)

W   **3–3**   **7–4**   **8–5–2**
                        7–4

Leaving the man on point 21 will cause problems for black. If black rolls any 6, white will find he has a shot. Consider how easy it would be for black if white's blot on point 21 were not there.

B   **4–3**   **19–23**   **20–23**

This leaves as few shots as possible.

W   **5–5**   **21–16–11–6–1**

White should be sure to leave the blot on point 8 alone. If white plays 21–16–11–6 8–3, he will be at the position shown below. If he rolls a 6 on his next turn, he will have to use a man on point 18. This will leave a shot somewhere. If, however, white still has a man on point 8, he will be able to play a 6 from point 8 to point 2. This play will hopefully enable white to outlast black in the waiting game to see who gives the first shot. At least white will manage to gain some time.

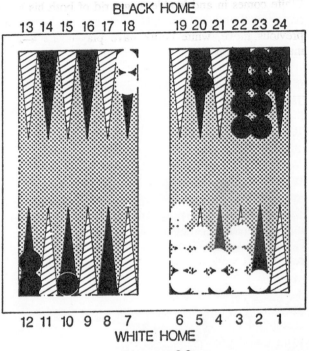

Diagram 8.2

B 4–3 10–13–17

Black might also play 20–23 20–24. The actual play, however, leaves only eleven ways to hit. Notice that white has two blots on his board, and black may have

53

a chance to hit one of them on his way in should white hit black on his next roll. The number of blots on the opponent's board is often a consideration when a player is thinking of leaving a shot. Black's alternative play leaves white with only 6–2, 5–3, and 4–4, or five ways to hit. However, playing in this way leaves black exposed to continuing problems. The potential problems of playing 20–23 20–24, plus white's blots on points 1 and 2 suggest the move as recorded.

W   **6–4**   **8–2**   **5–1**
A closed board.

B   **6–4**   **17–23**   **20–24**
Black definitely does not want to get hit now!

W   **4–1**   **6–2–1**
White is lucky that this roll did not break his board or force him to run from point 18. This is a fairly frequent situation in which each player waits and hopes for the first shot.

B   **5–3**   **12–17–20**
At this stage, if white hits (he has 17/36 chances), he is the winner. If white misses, black will double, and white will fold (with the possible exception of white's rolling 5–5 or 4–4). This next roll is probably the last pertinent roll of the game.

W   **5–3**
Black reaches for the doubling cube before white can play, and white concedes.

GAME 3

W   **6–2**   **13–7–5**

This is the aggressive way to play 6–2. The other ways are: 24–18   13–11, a good way. And 24–18–16, a poor way.

B   **3–1**   **1–2–5X**

Black could make his 20 (5) point, but it is better to keep white from making his own 5 point, even at the sacrifice of using a 3–1.

W   **6–3**   **B–22–16**

White must use the 3 to come in. The 6 is played 22–16 because it leaves fewer shots than any other 6 (with the exception of 8–2, which also leaves fewer shots, but there is no future in acquiring the 2 point). Notice what has happened as a result of black's having hit white on the last roll. White is unable to do anything with this roll, and now black is in a position to make white's 5 point. White, on the other hand, has neither his 5 point nor a very good position. White's position is poor because he rolled a 6 when he came in with the 3. There was just no way to play the 6. There are, of course, 11/36 ways to roll a 6, and all of them are bad for white in positions of this kind. Remember this situation.

B   **2–1**   **1–3–4**

Normally, black would play 12–14 and either 1–2 or 19–20. White's man on point 16, however, puts too much pressure on point 14 should black play 12–14.

55

Even though a player should not make a habit of putting blots on the opponent's 4 or 5 points, it is not unreasonable here because there are blots on *both* the 4 and 5 points. If white does get a good roll, such as 3–1, which points to the blot on point 5, black can hope to come in with any 4, 3–1, 2–2, or 1–1. Any of these rolls will make the 4 point, giving black a good position.

W   6–4   13–7–3
White could play 16–10–6. 16–10   8–4X might lead to a fast win if the player is lucky.

B   2–1   4–5   19–21
Black makes the 5 point. Slotting 19–21 is better than slotting 12–14 because if the blot lasts, more can be accomplished at 21 than at 14.

W   4–2   8–4   6–4

B   5–3   17–22   19–22

W   6–4   13–7–3

B   4–1   12–16X   21–22
Probably 21–22 is wrong. It is safe, but it tends to burn a man. The third man on point 22 will seldom be of much use. Better to leave it on 21 in an effort to make the 21 (4) point. Black might not try this move, unless he has white's 5 point.

W   6–3   0
This is most unlucky. Only 4/36 numbers stay off.

B   6–3   5–11–14

If black had not played 21–22, he could now make the 21 (4) point.

W   6–4   **B–21–15**
The 4 is forced. Which must come in with it.

B   5–3   **12–15X**   **14–19**

W   5–4   **B–20–16X**
White could make the 20 (5) point. This move may buy some time.

B   2–2   **B–2**   **12–14–16X**   **15–17**

W   5–1   **B–20**   6–5X
This is potentially a fine roll for white. If black comes in with a poor number (such as 6–1 or 5–1) or if he doesn't come in at all, white will be in position to run black off the board.

B   6–4   Ø

W   **Double**

B   **Resign**
Black might accept this double if he didn't have a blot on point 16. If there were no blot, he could continue play.

GAME 4

B   6–1   12–18   17–18

W   4–2   8–4   6–4

B   6–1   12–18   19–20

This is the aggressive alternative to playing 1–2.

W   6–4   24–20X–14

White very much wanted to hit that man to stop black from making four points in a row.

B   6–5   B–5   12–18

Black would play B–5–11, but white has the extra man on point 14 that threatens the 11 point.

W   6–3   14–8–5X

Sometimes shots like this are overlooked.

B   6–5   B–5X–11

This time black can play 6–5 the way discussed before because white's blot on point 14 is gone.

W   5–3   B–22   13–8

It would be dangerous for white to come in with B–20. White does not want to get hit on point 20 where black might make a point. As a general principle, a player should not put a blot on a point if the opponent can put a point on there.

B   3–3   19–22X   18–21
                              19–22   18–21

White is in deep trouble.

W   5–4   B–20   24–20

This excellent number will probably keep black from doubling.

| B | 5–2 | 11–16–18 | |

| W | 3–1 | 8–5 | 6–5 |

| B | 3–1 | 18–21 | 1–2 |

| W | 5–3 | 13–8–5 | |

13–8 13–10 might have been better. Even though black split his back men, only 6–3 or 5–4 can hit a blot on point 10.

| B | 6–6 | 12–18–24 | |
| | | 12–18–24 | |

6–6 isn't so good for black. Notice black did not play 12–18 17–23, 12–18 17–23.

| W | 3–2 | 6–3 | 5–3 |

| B | 3–1 | 18–19 | 18–21 |

Black is getting himself far too advanced.

| W | 4–2 | 20–18 | 20–16 |

This leaves only 1's with which black can hit—11/36 chances. White can instead play 13–11 13–9. This move also has 11/36 chances. These shots are (see the next diagram) 6–6, 6–5, 6–4, 6–2, 5–4, and 5–2. The objection to this play is that if black gets one blot, he may have time to get one or both of the other ones.

One more possibility for this 4–2 roll is to play 8–6 8–4. This move is certainly safe, but it may lead to future problems. Any roll totaling 6 or less will leave a shot. The last and most aggressive play is

8–4–2X. With reasonable luck, this move can lead to a gammon. If, incidentally, the reader thinks that white should have doubled on this or on a preceding roll, he is quite right. White's handling of the cube in this game has been poor. (See section on doubling.)

BLACK HOME

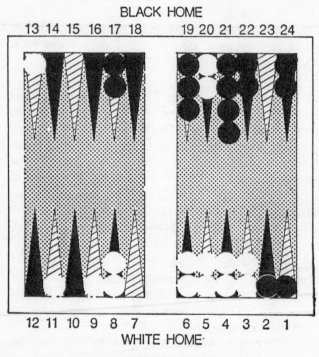

Diagram 8.3

B   **6–5**   **1–7**   **2–7**
Super roll. It stops white from making a prime, and it

releases the back men, and both safely. It also gives white second thoughts about doubling.

W	6–4	18–12	16–12
B	2–1	21–23	17–18
W	4–1	13–9–8	
B	5–2	19–24	21–23

At this moment, white has the better position, although he is trailing by 26 pips. Notice that black did not bring in a man from 17 or 18. He is keeping them to use in case he rolls a 6. Black intends to wait as long as possible before leaving the 7 point. He may either get a shot or he may roll some number that lets him advance the back men together (3–3, 2–2, or 4–4).

W	5–5	13–8–3
		13–8–3

This is a good running number. As a rule, 5–5 is good only during the running game and is certainly good for that play here.

B	5–1	17–22–23	
W	6–1	8–2	3–2
B	4–1	19–23–24	

Black is still keeping the man on point 18 to take care of 6's.

W	5–4	8–3	8–4
B	5–3	18–21	19–24
W	5–4	6–1	6–2
B	6–4	7–13	7–11

The 4 is played to cut down on the chances of white's hitting. This way black leaves only 1's with which white can hit. White has 11/36 chances to hit. If black had played 7–13–17, white would have been able to hit with any 5, 4–1 and 3–2, or 15/36 ways.*

| W | 6–3 | 12–9 | 12–6 |

Now it's just a running game.

| B | 6–2 | 11–13–19 | |
| W | 5–4 | 9–5–0 | |

| B | 3–1 | 13–16 | 19–20 |

13–16–17 was an alternative. The way used avoids misses should a 5 be rolled before a 6.

W	4–3	4–0	3–0
B	3–1	16–19	24–0
W	6–4	6–0	4–0
B	5–4	20–0	21–0

*More on this position in the section on positions.

W	4–2	4–0	2–0
B	6–3	19–0	22–0

W	4–3	5–1	3–0

White cannot take a man off with the 4, so he uses it to bring a man to the 1 point. White would like no more 4's for awhile.

B	1–1	24–0
		24–0
		24–0
		24–0

W	6–2	5–0	2–0

When bearing off, if a player rolls a number that is higher than the highest numbered blot on his board, he may bear off that highest numbered blot. Here white rolled a 6, but there are no men on the 6 point. The next highest numbered blot is 5, so it is taken off instead.

B	6–5	21–0	21–0

Ditto . . . twice.

W	4–3	3–0	3–0

Ditto. After white plays his 4–3, we have the position in the following diagram. Black rolls next. Black will win unless he rolls a 1 on either of his next turns or if white rolls any doubles on his turn. Should black double? This and other positions will be discussed in the section on the doubling cube.

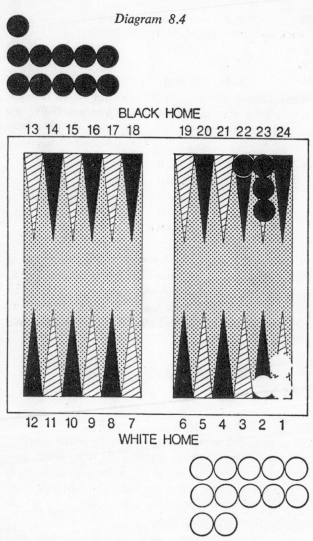

Diagram 8.4

BLACK HOME

13 14 15 16 17 18   19 20 21 22 23 24

12 11 10 9 8 7   6 5 4 3 2 1

WHITE HOME

64

B　　　　6–1　　　22–0　　　23–24

Black does not want to see that one.

W　　　　**Double**

B　　　　**Resign**

Black had the game won until he rolled that 6–1. Now he needs double 2 or higher to win, but he doesn't get to try because white doubles. Black can't afford to accept this double.

GAME 5

W　　　　2–1　　　13–11　　　6–5

More aggressive than 13–11　24–23.

B　　　　6–2　　　12–14–20

With white having a blot on point 11, black can't consider the alternative play of 12–14　1–7.

W　　　　4–2　　　24–20X　　　13–11

This move is in keeping with the general strategy of not letting the opponent make his 5 point. Normally one would play 8–4　6–4 making his 4 point.

B　　　　5–1　　　B–5X　　　19–20X

Black hits, coming in with the 5, and he hits 19–20X since it starts his 20 (5) point and sends two enemy men back. Black would like to see white roll a 6 on his next roll. White could then bring only one man in, and black might be able to begin an attack.

W	5–2	B–20X	B–23

B	5–3	B–5	12–15

Not B–3 12–17. Making the 5 point is a must. Nor does black care if 15 gets hit by 20 because white won't be able to make the 20 (5) point. An excellent alternative is B–5 17–20X, since it stops white from making the 20 (5) point.

W	3–1	24–23–20

B	6–3	12–18	15–18

W	6–3	23–20–14

Escape?

B	5–4	5–9–14X

No escape.

W	6–4	B–21	20–14X

B	2–1	B–2	19–20X

Black shouldn't bother making the 2 point. Hitting is far better since it keeps the pressure on white.

W	6–5	B–20X	11–5X

This play hits two men. If black rolls a 6 on his next roll, he will be able to bring in only one man. White may then be able to make his 5 point while black still has a man off. This position is almost exactly the same as black had just a few rolls earlier. Hitting two men can be an extremely strong play.

B	6–3	B–3	Ø

The game is now as shown in this diagram.

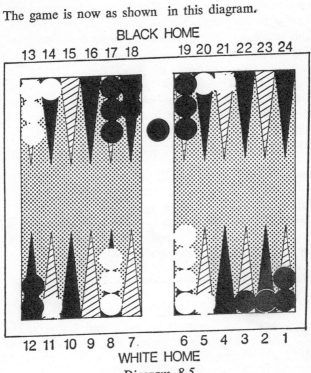

BLACK HOME

13 14 15 16 17 18   19 20 21 22 23 24

12 11 10 9 8 7   6 5 4 3 2 1

WHITE HOME

Diagram 8.5

This may be a crucial point of the game. Black's 6–3 was bad. A man stayed off and black missed the blot on point 5. White now has a large number of good rolls. White may be able to make his 5 point, his opponents 20 (5) point, or both. Or perhaps white can pick up one or more additional black blots.

W   5–5   20–15–10–5   8–3X

This move keeps two men on the bar and makes the 5

point as well. Notice that 5–5 can bring a man from one 5 point to the other (barring black's blocking points). This fact has been overlooked by more than one good player. Remember it.

B   5–2   **B–2**   ∅
Black is not too unhappy because he has two points now. This position can be played by black for quite a while.

W   6–3   6–3   14–8
Better is 13–7, going for the bar point.

B   4–2   **B–4**   2–4
Black shouldn't play B–2   17–21X. He needs the 4 point to keep alive. If he stays on the 1 and 2 points, the position will be too cramped too soon.

W   6–2   21–15–13

B   5–1   2–7   19–20
Black has a back game with the 1 and 4 points. He won't mind being hit now since it will help him to slow down his progress.

W   6–2   11–5–3
White now regrets not having slotted a man on the bar on either of his previous rolls.

B   2–2   17–19–21   18–20   12–14
The 12–14 is an effort to be hit and therefore to gain time.

W   5–2   13–8–6

B   6–5   14–20   17–22

Black would prefer smaller numbers. He wants to build a board in anticipation of getting a shot at white later. But if he goes too fast, he may lose his good board by the time he gets his shot. If this happens, the value of having a shot will be greatly diminished.

W   4–1   6–2   3–2

Definitely not playing 13–12X–8. White does not want to give black that extra time he needs to build and to *keep* his board.

B   5–1   17–22   20–21

Black's board is becoming formidable. White may be in trouble if he can't get his men down safely.

Black played his 5–1 by making two points on his board. He did not play 7–12 to pick up his blots. If he had wanted to do that he would have picked them up long ago, or perhaps not have left them in the first place. Look at the position closely. Black has single blots on the 7 and 12 points, which are very painful to white. But they are painful only because black holds white's 1 and 4 points. Now, if white hits one of black's blots, black will have two things going for him:

1. Black may get a return shot on the next roll (unlikely).
2. Black will be able to slow down the advance of his men. He has four important points on his board. Now if white hits a blot, it will effectively give black "time" or "tempo" to keep those points intact. This way if black later picks up a white blot, he will be able to make something of it.

69

This diagram shows the current position.

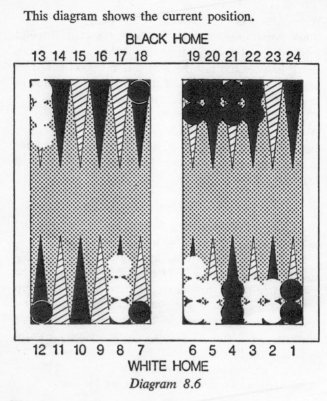

BLACK HOME

13 14 15 16 17 18   19 20 21 22 23 24

12 11 10 9 8 7   6 5 4 3 2 1

WHITE HOME

Diagram 8.6

W   6–3   13–7X   8–5

The alternative is 8–2 6–3. It is safe, but it leaves an awkward position. White would just as soon not have to hit.

B   5–4   B–4   18–23

The man on point 12 remains as a threat should white bring only one man down from point 13. If 12 gets hit, it will slow black down.

70

W   **5–1**   **13–12X–7**

White hits because he can't afford to leave the blot there as a threat to point 13.

B   **6–5**   Ø

W   **4–4**   **13–9–5**   **7–3**
                                                7–3

This roll is not quite as good as it looks. 6–6, 6–1, 6–4, 5–1, and 5–4 all leave shots. This is one of the few times 4–4 is not a good roll.

B   **5–3**   Ø

W   **6–4**   **8–2**   **6–2**

Not best for white. Black now has a shot, albeit a poor one. Black hits with 4–1 or 4–4.

B   **3–1**   **B–1–4**

At this stage white will be very lucky not to leave a shot. Black has two extra men on point 4, so he has good tempo.

W   **6–2**   **8–6–0**

B   **4–1**   **4–8–9**

Notice that 6–5, 6–2, 5–4, and 4–2 all leave shots, double shots at that.

W   **6–4**   **6–0**   **6–2**

Excellent roll.

B   **5–3**   **9–14–17**

71

W   4–2   2–0   ∅

There is no way to play the 4.

B   5–4   4–8–13

W   5–3   5–0   3–0

B   6–3   17–23   13–16

Black is ready with his reception committee, hopefully.

W   6–5   6–0   5–0

Black now has a double shot. He can hit with 1's and 4's, or 20/36 times. Black can't double yet because white would take the double and then double back if black missed the shot. Black could not take the double.

B   6–2   16–22–24

Black may justifiably be disappointed. White may now double—a move black should pass—or white may play for a gammon. Only 4–4, 4–1, and 2–2 will cause problems for white now.

W   3–1   5–2   3–2

White does not consider taking a man off. It would leave a shot.

B   3–1   4–7   4–5

W   **Double**

White's last roll is not what he had hoped. In this position 6–2, 5–2, 4–2, 3–2, and 2–1 leave shots. Further considerations of this position may be found in the section on doubling.

B　　　**Resign**

GAME 6

W	5–1	13–8	6–5

B	2–2	1–3–5X	19–21
			19–21

Always hit that blot on point 5 in this situation. 1–1 is about the only roll one might not use for that purpose.

W	6–4	Ø

B	6–1	12–18	17–18

W	3–2	B–22	24–22

With black making his bar point, it is important for white to own one of the advanced points on black's board. This way, white can escape with 6–6, something he can't do from 24.

B	5–3	12–17	12–15

Black might run 5–10　12–15, but he wants to make his 20 (5) point if he can. That extra builder on point 17 is important.

73

W	3–1	8–5X	6–5

B	5–3	B–3	12–17

Black has to come in with the 3. His 5, however, is no bargain. 12–17 here looks like the least bad play. White can hit with any 1, 5–2, 5–4, and 6–4—or 17/36 times. If black plays his 5 from 15 to 20 instead, he will be vulnerable to any 2's, 4's, and 3–1—or 22/36 times.

W	6–5	13–7	8–3X

This is dangerous and one shouldn't try it except that white holds a point on black's board. If white does get hit, he may come in with a 1, giving him black's 24 (1) point. He will then have a good back game.

B	4–4	B–4	15–19–23
			19–23

W	4–2	7–3	6–4X

Other moves were:

13–11–7. This makes the bar point, but does not hit a man.

8–4X 6–4. This makes the 4 point and it hits a man, but it leaves blots on the 3, 7, and 8 points (see the next diagram).

24–20 22–20. This does very little; it doesn't hit and therefore gives black time to improve his position. . . . Black will be delighted if white does not hit him. By hitting, white may be able to get the blot on point 12 if black can't save it.

74

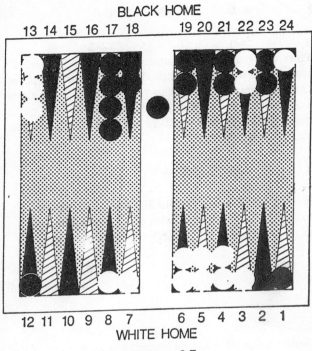

12 11 10 9 8 7   6 5 4 3 2 1

WHITE HOME

Diagram 8.7

B   6–2   **B–2**   12–18

W   2–1   4–2X–1X

Hitting two men here may gain quite a bit of time. Black will stay out with both men 9/36 times. He will come in with only one man 18/36 times. He will come in with both men 9/36 times.

75

B	6–1	B–1X	Ø

W	2–1	B-24	22–20

White plays 22–20 to increase his option. 24–22 is wrong because it leaves a "candlestick" of men on point 22, which may be difficult to remove later. Since black is on the bar, there is not much he can do to hurt white at this point. Only 4–4, 2–2, and 1–1 can be played effectively for black.

B	5–4	B-4-9

W	3–1	13–10–9X

B	2–2	B–2	18–20X
	17–19		
			18–20

Joker! It comes in, hits, and builds a crucial point, all at once.

W	6–3	B–22	24–18X

Return joker. If white had rolled a poor number, black would have doubled, which would have ended the game.

B	6–1	B–1–7

W	6–5	13–7X–2X

If this works out for white, he will double.

B	5–1	B–1	Ø

White would have preferred black not to roll a 1.

W	4–2	8–4–2

B   **4–3**   **B–4**   **1–4**

Another game saver. This game has had a number of
spectacular rolls on both sides to save what looked like
lost positions. That's backgammon!

W   **5–1**   **18–13**   **9–8**

Black rolls with the game in the position shown in this
diagram. How should black play 6–1?

BLACK HOME

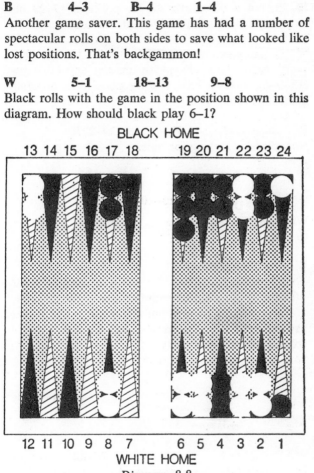

Diagram 8.8

B   **6–1**   **19–20**   **1–7**

1–7 hopes to escape. Black can make the safe play of

77

17–23, but it does little for his position. 17–23 also uses one of black's builders for little reason.

W   **4–1**   **8–7X**   **22–18**
White isn't all that happy to hit, but any other play (13–9–8) leaves a blot. Hitting gains time, hopefully, but it's nervous.

B   **4–2**   **B–4**   **20–22X**
Now black is looking for time.

W   **6–4**   **0**

B   **Double**
When white did not come in, the time factor went over to black.

W   **Resign**
There are too many blots for white to consider taking. White might find himself wth five men on the bar.

An interesting thing about this game is that if black had not come in on the previous roll, white would probably have won quite easily.

GAME 7

B   **6–3**   **1–7–10**

W   **5–2**   **13–8**   **24–22**
13–11 is bad because black has a direct shot with the man on point 10.

B   **4–2**   **9–14**   **12–14**

A reasonable alternative is 17–21   19–21, making the 21 (4) point.

W	6–2	13–7–5	
B	4–4	1-5X–9	14–18
			14–18

As before, black should hit a blot on white's 5 point at the expense of using an otherwise good roll.

W	5–5	B–20	13–8–3
			8–3

B	6–3	9–12–18

Black can play 9–15   12–15, but this gives him a point he may later wish he didn't have. The actual play improves his chances of getting all his men home without mishap.

W	4–2	8–4	22–20

White has a large number of possible choices. They are:

1. 8–4   6–4. This makes his 4 point but leaves his back men in danger. It is crucial for white to make the 20 (5) points.

2. 24–20   6–4. This makes the important 20 (5) point. But there is a major difference in this play and the actual play. Look at Diagram 8.9 and compare it with the position on your board. The difference between the two positions is the blot on point 22 or point 24. On which point should one leave the blot? In these situations, that blot on point 24 makes all the difference! It keeps black

79

from being able to drop men indiscriminately on his inner board. The blot on 24 will force black to look elsewhere for places to play rolls that he could easily play onto his board if point 24 were not there. If the blot were on point 22, the effect would be seriously diminished.

3. 24–20 22–20. From the above discussion, it should be clear that white must not make

BLACK HOME

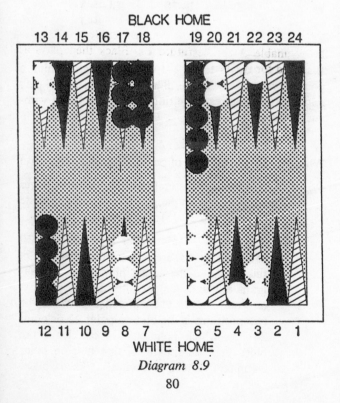

Diagram 8.9

80

this play. Doing so would make it far too easy for black to bring his men in, and white is too far behind in the race to permit black this comfort.

B   6–2   12–18   19–21

Already white's last play is paying dividends. If white had not left that man on point 24, black could make this play with impunity. As it is, black has an unpleasant decision to make. Probably black will have to make some more unpleasant decisions. Here, black can play safe for the moment with 12–18 17–19. This, however, strips the 17 point of builders and leaves black unable to handle future 2's. Black then plays as indicated for two reasons:

1. If the blot does not get hit, black will probably be able to cover it on his next roll. The addition of the 21 (4) point should make it much easier for him to bring his men in.

2. A general principle of backgammon is: When one expects that he will have to take a shot or shots, it is often best to give a shot before the opponent's board can be developed. In this case, white has a poor board, and a blot in it as well. However, it has the potential for fast improvement. Black does not wish to be hit, but if it must happen, black would rather try to come onto this white board than on the board white expects to have after a few more rolls.

W   3–1   24–21X-20

White shouldn't pick up 4 since it's the start of his 4

point. If it gets hit, white can hope to roll a 1 or even a 2, which will again harass black's entry onto his board.

| B | 5–3 | B–5 | 18–21 |

| W | 3–1 | 8–5X–4 |

8–5X   6–5 is a good alternative.

| B | 6–2 | B–2–8X |

| W | 4–3 | B–21X | 6–3 |

| B | 6–3 | ∅ |

| W | 5–2 | 13–8X | 13–11 |

13–11 instead of 6–4, because white wants to make the 5 point. 13–11 increases his chances.

| B | 4–2 | B–2 | ∅ |

| W | 5–3 | 20–15 | 11–8 |

The man on point 21 is left for whatever amount of harassment it can generate.

| B | 5–2 | B–5 | 19–21X |

| W | 4–3 | B–21X | 8–5X |

This is a strong roll for white.

| B | 3–2 | B–2 | ∅ |

| W | **Double** |

Cube from 1 to 2.

B   **Accept**

Refer to section on doubles.

W	5–5	15–10–5	6–1
			6–1

B   5–2   B–2   12–17

Black has been reasonably lucky in re-entering. On the roll before, black came in with a 2 and was able to make the 2 point. Then on this roll black was able to come in again with a 2, since it was the only number with which he could re-enter.

W	5–3	8–5	21–16

B	5–3	2–7	18–21

W	3–1	16–13	5–4

B	6–2	7–13X	19–21

W	6–3	B–22–16

B   6–1   13–19   17–18

White was quite lucky not to be hit.

W	5–2	16–11–9

B	1–1	12–13–14
		12–13–14

W	6–4	20–16–10

B   5–2   2–7–9X

Black can hit in two places. His other play is 13–19

18–20X. The second play would leave the position in Diagram 8.10. Black does not wish to be hit now, since it could easily lead to a gammon for white. As it is, black will be in excellent shape *if* his actual play lives. The greatest danger is in getting hit on the 2 point if white rolls a number that includes a 1 or a 2, which will hit. Perhaps for this reason, if for no other, black should make the alternate play. For whatever it's worth, there was more controversy between good players on this play than on any other in this book.

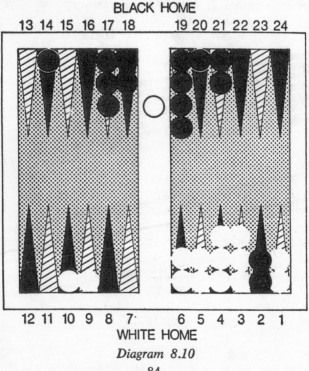

BLACK HOME

Diagram 8.10

W	6–4	Ø

B   **Double**
Cube from 2 to 4.

W   **Accept**
Refer to section on doubling.

B	4–1	9–10X–14	
W	3–2	B–22	B–23
B	2–1	18–20X	19–20
W	6–4	Ø	

This roll can be annoying.

B	5–2	2–7	17–19
W	3–2	B–22	4–2
B	4–4	7–11–15–19	14–18
W	6–1	23–22–16	

22–16 is the only 6. It is forced.

B   4–2   14–16X–20
For the moment, the black blot can't be hit.

W   3–1   B–22   3–2
White is ready, but it won't wait, unfortunately.

B   6–1   14–20–21

W	5–1	6–1	6–5

B	5–1	18–23–24	

W	5–3	5–2	Ø

White has no 5 to play.

B	3–1	20–21–24	

Black doesn't bring two men in because he wishes to keep white's men on point 22 just a while longer. Black would like to see white have to break up his board a bit more. He shouldn't play 19–20–23! 5–5 would leave a shot.

W	5–1	2–1	Ø

Still no 5's.

B	6–4	17–23	17–21

Notice that black can drop a man on point 23. If white had been able to maintain a blot on 23, black would not have enjoyed this 6–4.

W	6–2	22–16–14	

B	4–1	19–23	19–20

W	3–2	14–12–9	

B	4–4	19–23	20–24
		19–23	20–24

Doubles are frequently not too good in positions like this one.

86

W	2–2	22–20X	9–7–5
		22–20	

B	6–2	B-6–8

W	3–2	20–17	5–3

White shouldn't play the entire move inside his board because it would mean breaking a point. White intends (hopes) to hit black and needs to keep his board as intact as possible. Even if white gets hit, he can expect to come in and may even have a return shot.

B	6–5	18–23	18–24

8–13–19 is possible. It leaves 1's to hit, 11/36 ways. The actual play leaves 6–6, 6–3, 5–4, and 3–3 or 6/36 ways to hit.

W	5–4	17–13–8X

Lucky.

B	6–2	B-6–8X

Luckier!

W	2–1	∅

B	6–2	8–14	21–23

Black must play his 6 from 8 to 14, which reaches the position in Diagram 8.11. Black still has a 2 to play, which can be 21–23 or 14–16. If black leaves the blot on point 14, it can be hit by 6–6, 6–5, 6–3, and 3–3, or six ways. On the other hand, a blot left on point 16 can be hit by 6–4, 6–3, 5–4, 4–3, and 3–3, or nine ways.

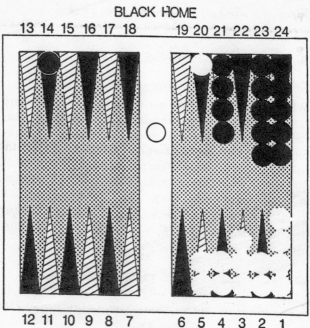

BLACK HOME

13 14 15 16 17 18   19 20 21 22 23 24

12 11 10 9 8 7   6 5 4 3 2 1

WHITE HOME

Diagram 8.11

| W | 3–3 | B–22 | 20-17-14X-11 |

White does not play B–22–19 to cater to the possibility of black rolling 6–6. By staying on point 22, white may get a later shot.

| B | 2–1 | ∅ |

| W | 4–2 | 22–20–16 |

| B | 3–2 | ∅ |

88

W	4–3	16–12	11–8

B	6–3	B–6–9

W **Double**
Cube from 4 to 8.

B **Accepts**
This is an easy accept. Black is actually ahead in the running game, although white has better distribution of men to bear off. White will hit the blot 14/36 times, which will cost black some time. Perhaps it will cost quite a bit of time. On the other hand, no one is going to get gammoned, and should white miss, black has quite good chances. It would be no surprise to see the cube come back at 16!

W	5–3	12–9X–4	

B	4–1	∅

W	4–1	8–4	1–0

B	4–2	∅

W	2–1	3–1–0

B	6–3	B–6–9

W	4–2	4–0	2–0

B	3–1	9–12–13

W	2–2	4–2–0
		4–2–0

Only two men can come off.

B	6–6	13–19–0	21–0
			21–0

W	4–2	4–0	2–0

White does not care for this 4–2. It leaves no men on either points 4 or 2 and rolls including these numbers will "miss" or fail to take a man off. Admittedly, white is not in serious trouble yet, but this is the way to get into it.

B	2–1	23–0	24–0

W	6–1	5–0	1–0

B	2–2	23–0
		23–0
		23–0
		23–0

The game is now as in Diagram 8.12. White rolls a 4–2.

W	4–2	5–3–0

Notice how white plays this roll. It looks like there is no other way, but look: 5–1 3–1—no man off. Both moves are legal, but only one of them is correct. By playing the first, 5–3, a man can be taken off by 3–0. But by the simple oversight of 5–1, no man comes off. Remember this situation. It's an easy one to overlook.

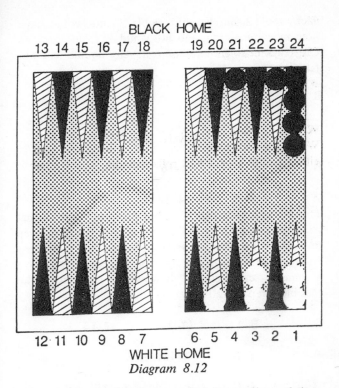

Diagram 8.12

A lot of fine players will agree wholeheartedly, and they will no doubt be happy to recall various sad stories when they lost such-and-such because of this mistake.

B	6–2	21–0	23–0

W	6–5	3–0	3–0

If, in this position, white had rolled a 2, black would be the favorite! In fact, black would double, and white would pass. If white had misplayed the previous roll, black would again have a double. White would have three men remaining, and he would have to pass. As it is, black does get one last roll. Any double will win it for him. So . . .

B ?

GAME 8

B	4–1	12–16	19–20

| **W** | 6–5 | 24–18–13 | |

This roll is nice to run with, but it is really not all that good. It does nothing to improve white's board or even to improve his chances. Even if he gets lucky and gets another 6–5, he won't be too well placed. He will have a game of "candlesticks." It would be far better to hit that blot on point 20 (5).

B	3–2	17–20	12–14

| **W** | 5–3 | 24–21–16X | |

B	1–1	B–1	14–15–16X
	19–20		

Black plays 19–20 instead of 1–2 because it greatly improves his chances of making a point on his board on the next roll. This way he has men on points 16, 17, 19, and 20, all working. The other way, he has men only on points 16, 17, and 19. 19–20 is far better than 1–2.

W	4–2	B–23	13–9

White doesn't come in B–21 because he is afraid of having a point put on his head. If black wants to make a point on white at 23 it's fine with white, but it's not good for white to have a black point on his head on point 21.

B   **4–2**   **12–16**   **1–3**

If white had played B–21 on the last roll . . . disaster! Black's 4–2 would execute him with 17–21   19–21.

W   **5–1**   **13–8**   **9–8**

There is no convenient move for white to take. 23–22, perhaps, but white doesn't wish to get pointed on 22. Nor is 8–7 or 6–5 to be considered because: 1) Black is attacking from two points, not just one, and 2) Black's board is likely to improve too fast to want to have any extra men back there.

B	**4–4**	**1–5**	**17–21**
		1–5	**17–21**

W   **5–4**   **23–18–14**

B   **6–3**   **5–11–14X**

White definitely did not want to get hit.

W   **6–4**   **0**

B   **Double**

Cube from 1 to 2.

W   **Accept**

Poor. See section on doubles.

93

BLACK HOME

13 14 15 16 17 18   19 20 21 22 23 24

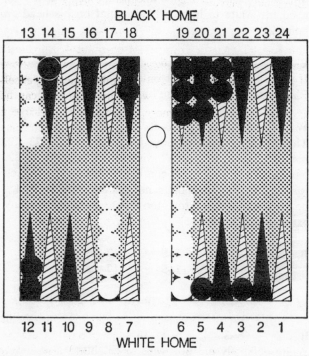

12 11 10 9 8 7   6 5 4 3 2 1

WHITE HOME

Diagram 8.13

The game now is as in Diagram 8.13.

W   5–1   **B–24**   **13–8**

White can't play 8-3X because it is too dangerous now to get hit again. As it is, he is going to have to find some way to get the blot on point 24 to safety. Perhaps he should not have accepted the double?

| B | 1–1 | 14–15–16–17–18 |

Black isn't playing 3–4–5 because he wants to make it as hard as possible for white to get his men around and in. White will not want to hit the blots on points 5 or 3, nor will he want to drop a blot on point 4. Playing in this way, black has essentially deprived white of his 3, 4, and 5 points. Only if white rolls something excellent like 3–1, 1–1, or 4–2, which make points, can he come in safely. Furthermore, if white tries to leave a blot on his outer board, black will have two men bearing on it instead of just one.

| W | 6–1 | 13–7 | 8–7 |
| B | 6–6 | 3–9–15 | 5–11–17 |

| W | 5–3 | 8–3 | 6–3 |

| B | 6–4 | 17–23 | 19–23 |

Black's blot on point 15 is safe.

| W | 3–2 | 24–22 | 8–5 |

At this point, if black rolls 4–2, making a prime, he wins. So white steps onto 22, hoping only to escape. His earlier reasons for not going to point 22 no longer matter.

| B | 6–2 | 15–21–23 |

Black might play 15–21 20–22X, but inasmuch as black is far ahead in the running game, he has decided to play safe, and not hit. Perhaps a bit cowardly. On the other hand, hitting may be the only way to lose the game. White might be able to hit black's blot and cover his 5 point as well. Not likely, admittedly, since 3–1, 3–2, or 3–3 are the only numbers that will do it.

W	5–5	22–17	7–2	8–3
			7–2	

White shouldn't play 13–8. These men are needed to
13–8
put pressure on black's checkers on point 12. (Diagram 8.14).

BLACK HOME

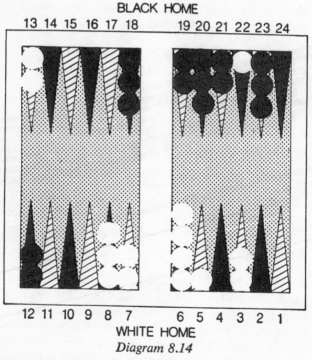

Diagram 8.14

B   6–2   18–24   20–22

Notice the problems black is having as a result of white's men on 13 and 17.

W   6–5   17–11–6

B   4–2   12–16   12–14

W   6–1   13–7   13–12

B   3–2   16–19   18–20

W   1–1   8–7–6   7–6–5

White would like fewer men on point 6.

B   4–2   14–18–20

W   4–3   12–9   8–4

White brings a man in to the 4 point. He could bring one in to the 5 point, but that would be silly. Better to try for some balance of distribution. As a rule, one wants to bring men in as quickly as possible. This situation is a mild exception.

B   2–1   18–19   23–0

W   5–2   9–4   2–0

B   2–1   23–0   24–0

W   2–1   3–2–0

B	4–4	21–0	19–23	20–24
		21–0		

W	4–3	4–0	3–0

B	5–1	20–0	24–0

W	6–3	6–0	3–0

B	6–4	19–0	20–24

W	4–4	4–0	6–2	5–1
			6–2	

Only one man comes off.

B	6–5	19–0	20–0

W	6–5	6–0	5–0

B	2–2	23–0	19–21–23
		23–0	

W	2–2	2–0	6–4
		2–0	
		2–0	

B	6–3	22–0	23–0

W	3–3	6–3–0	4–1–0

White needed 4–4 or better!

This is not one of the more exciting games in this section, but it had its points. It broke down into a running game rather early. As soon as contact between the men was terminated, the only problem was to get them onto and off the board as quickly as possible. It's more important to get the men in quickly, rather than neatly —although neatly, or well spread out, helps when one has a choice.

Look at the position in Diagram 8.15. If black rolls a 3–2, he should bring both men in to the 19 (6) point. He should not play 16–18   17–20. This play leaves a man outside, one that could have been brought in.

BLACK HOME

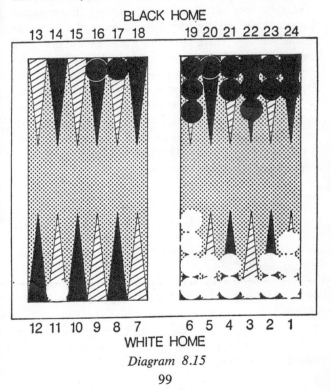

Diagram 8.15

If however, black rolls 3–1, he should play 17–20 16–17. As long as only one man is coming in on this roll, it is reasonable to play it to end up with as balanced a distribution of men as possible.

If it seems that some of the doubles and takes in the first eight games have been poor . . . well, some of them have. I suggest that for the most part, you do not attempt to draw any conclusions from the fact that someone did or did not double in a certain position. Instead, for purposes of learning and understanding the cube, refer only to the section on doubling. These games are concerned mainly with how to move the pieces to best advantage. There are times when the ownership of the cube may influence someone to make a play that he would not make if the opponent owned the cube, but for now, that consideration is purposely being ignored.

Handling of the cube, incidentally, is the most difficult and controversial part of the game. Often, two excellent players will disagree, and sometimes they will disagree quite violently. This fact will, as you play, become more and more apparent.

GAME 9

This is an extremely long game. If pressed for time, try another.

B	4–1	12–16	19–20

W	3–1	24–21–20X	

White shouldn't play 8–5 6–5. No one gets a 5 point this way, but he has sent a man back.

B   6–5   B–5   16–22

Black might play 5–11, but the blot on point 20 hits with any 8 by white's blot on 20, as well as by any 2 from the 13 point.

W   3–1   8–5X   6–5

B   4–2   B–4   22–24X

There is no decent 2 to play. Hitting may cause white to lose the benefit of a good roll such as 3–1 or 4–2.

W   **Double**

Cube from 1 to 2.

B   **Accept**

W   1–1   B–24X   6–5–4X   8–7

This is a joker for white. It hits two men and threatens to build an instant board. With two men on the bar, white can safely play 8–7, which he might not do if black had only one man on the bar.

B   6–3   B–3   ∅

W   4–2   6–4   7–3X

Keeping up the pressure!

B   4–1   B–1   ∅

W   6–4   13–7–3

B   4–4   ∅

W   6–2   13–11   13–7

B	5–3	∅
W	5–1	11–6	8–7
B	6–2	B–2–8

The position is now as in Diagram 8.16.

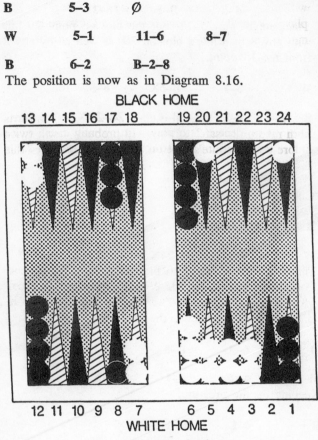

Diagram 8.16

| W | 4–2 | 24–22 | 20–16 |

White has three ways to take this 4–2: 24–20   6–4,
20–16–14, and 24–22   20–16. The first will not
play for him if he subsequently rolls 3–3 or 1–1. 3–3

will force him to run with the men on point 13. This play will make it awkward for him to get those last two men home. If he rolls 1–1, he will have to either leave a shot in his board or he will have to give up one of his points. The second way won't leave him with any embarrassing rolls, but he will have a blot on point 14 that can be hit with relative impunity. He will, if hit, be lucky to hit back. The third play, 24–22 20–16, starts both men off to safety. Black will probably think twice before hitting white's blot on point 16 if he takes this play. Certainly, it will be harder for black to find satisfactory moves.

B   **4–3**   **12–16X**   **19–22X**

This roll may give black enough time to do something about his board.

W   **5–1**   **B–20**   **B–24**

If black had not hit two men the roll before, white would be able to hit black now with 13–8X.

B   **4–4**   **8–12–16–20X**
                        16–20

W   **5–3**   **B–22X**   **13–8**

This roll brings this up to position in Diagram 8.17. White has come in on point 22, putting black on the bar, and has played 13–8. 13–8 was almost forced, since the other 5 would be silly. The interesting point about this position is the relative safety of white's blot on 13. It looks, at first glance, as though black could hit it with any 1. Black, however, has a man on the bar and only two numbers will bring it in—1 and 20. It turns out that black can hit with only 3/36 numbers,

2–1 and 1–1. In all the other numbers containing a 1, black has to use the 1 to come in. He can't use it to hit.

This is a good concept to notice and remember. If the opponent has a man on the bar that can come in with only certain numbers, a player may sometimes leave shots that can be hit only with the same numbers as are needed by the opponent to come in. In this case, the opponent needs a 1 or a 2. So white has left him an outside shot requiring one of those numbers—1. Admittedly, this play was, in fact, almost forced, but the point of this situation is well worth noting.

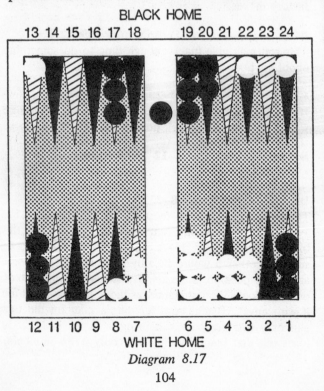

BLACK HOME

Diagram 8.17

B	6–4	∅	
W	3–2	13–11	24–21

This move is far more important than it might at first seem. There are in fact two other that might have some appeal, but they are traps that can lead to disasterous results. The other moves are:

1. 13–10–8. This makes a 6 point prime and looks quite nice. But look at what happens if on the next roll white is not able to play with one of his two back men. Say he rolls 5–2, or even worse—5–3, 3–3, or 5–5. He will have to break up his prime, and he may even have to leave a shot. And if he finds himself stuck back there on his next roll as well, he will probably lose what now appears to be a sure game.

2. 24–22 13–10. This possibility also has certain hazards. Any combination of 2's, 3's, and 5's will find white in danger of losing his good board. And if he rolls badly for two or even three times in a row, he is in trouble. But look what happens if he makes the play of 13–11 24–21. Now he can get out of there with 6's, 5's, 4's, and 3's. The numbers that don't let him out are 1's and 2's, and he probably will be able to handle quite a few of them before anything bad happens to his position.

In order for black to do white any harm, he is going to have to roll a 2 followed by a 6. If he can do this, white may not get his prime. However, the danger to white of getting his back checkers stuck is far greater than the danger of black getting a 2 and 6 before white can close the prime.

Even if black does manage that 2 or 6, he will have to

get his other men out. This can be done only if black rolls 1's followed by 6's. White expects to have a lot of time to get his work done. One last consideration is that if black does manage to get a 1, and moves 1–2 in an effort to escape, white may be able to hit him.

B	5–1	B–1	12–17

W	3–1	11–8	22–21

After the last discussion, it should be clear that white should have played 11–8 6–5. This play leaves more numbers for those men in back to escape.

B	5–2	17–19	17–22

W	4–3	21–18–14

B	4–2	20–22	20–24

This is a very poor move. The only reason to make it was that it did not leave a blot. There are two other moves, however, which have quite a bit of appeal. They are:

1. 17–21X 19–21. The result of this move is shown in Diagram 8.18. If white does not come in or if he comes in without hitting, black may be able to contain the white blot and force white to break up his prime. In this hypothetical position, white comes in with, say 4–2. He plays B–23 and 14–10. Black gets lucky and rolls 6–3, which plays 16–22X 19–22. White comes in with, say, a 5–1, and plays B–24 10–5. Now, regard-

13 14 15 16 17 18   19 20 21 22 23 24

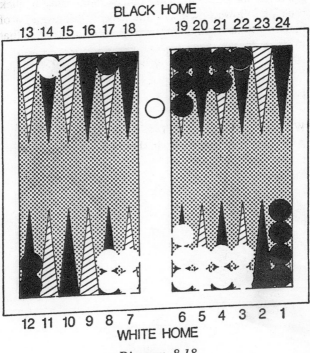

12 11 10 9 8 7   6 5 4 3 2 1

WHITE HOME

Diagram 8.18

less of what black rolls, white will be in trouble if he rolls 4–4. Even if white gets away from the trap, black will have a good chance to recapture the man and send it back.

Going back to the real position in Diagram 8.19, black may consider playing his 4–2 this way: 17–21X 12–14X

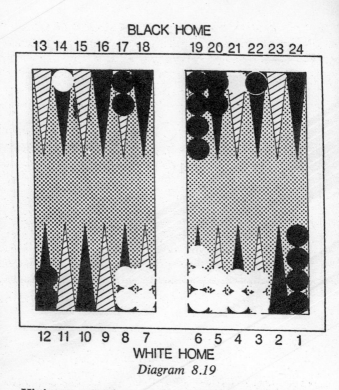

13 14 15 16 17 18   19 20 21 22 23 24

12 11 10 9 8 7   6 5 4 3 2 1

WHITE HOME
Diagram 8.19

Hitting two men leaves the position in Diagram 8.20, not a common position to be sure. It has quite a few things going for it, though. These rolls are terrible for white. 6–6, 5–5, and 6–5 don't bring a man in.

6–1, 6–2, 5–1, and 5–2 bring only one checker in, and they don't hit either black blot. This is a total of twelve very bad rolls for white. These rolls all give black good chances to force white to break up his board. Additionally, 3–3, which brings both men in, also forces white to break up the prime right now!

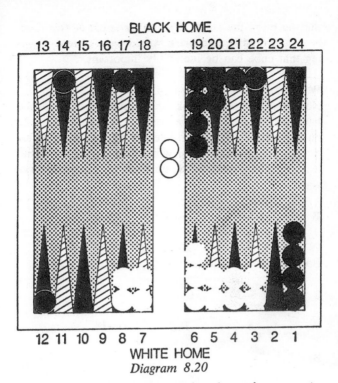

Diagram 8.20

If white elects to try one of the alternative ways to play this 4–2, and it doesn't work, he can hope. Even if he gets away, and especially if he hits one or more of black's blots in the process, he has a chance. I'll go into the end game later in the section on situations. Black's chances are better than one would think. Admittedly, he won't prove to be the favorite, but he will have definite chances to win.

There is one last point to make at this moment. Why is black able to play at all in this game? The answer is that he owns the cube. If white owned it at this time, he would double, and black would have to fold. Owning that cube can be incredibly important.

W	2–2	8–6–4	6–4–2

Not good for white. Look what would have happened had black elected to put a point on white's blot on 21 on the last roll. As it is, white has elected to try to re-establish his prime. True, white can play the roll and leave no blots, but ensuing numbers may become awkward.

B	3–1	1–2X	19–22

W	5–2	B–20	4–2X

Both players want to get that 2 point desperately.

B	5–3	∅	

W	5–2	7–2	20–18

B	4–2	∅	

W	2–1	8–7	18–16

Black doesn't mind not coming in now. Hopefully, when he eventually hits a blot, he will be able to make use of it. In order to do this, he will need to have some semblance of a board remaining at that time. For these same reasons, black would like to see white go faster. If white keeps rolling little numbers, black will, in the meantime, be advancing his men. If they become too far advanced, as discussed earlier, it will do black no good to hit one of white's pieces.

110

B	3–3	∅

W	1–1	21–20	16–15–14–13

B   6–2   ∅

Black is not bothered by staying out. He will either win the game, or he will get gammoned. Coming in now is less likely to help save the gammon than it is to hurt black's chances of actually winning the game.

W	4–3	20–16–13

Mistake. White should play 20–16 14–11. As played, 1–1 will be embarrassing.

B   6–6   ∅

Black is quite pleased not to have to play this number.

W	5–5	13–8	14–9–4
		13–8	

B   3–2   ∅

W	5–3	7–2	7–4

This is a common end position in backgammon. Look at Diagram 8.21. One's first impulse may be to play 8–3 8–5, but this time, instinct is wrong. If white plays 8–3 8–5, he will find himself in the position of Diagram 8.22. Now if he rolls a 6–4 or 6–5, he will have to leave a direct shot. Or, he may roll any number, including a 6 followed by another number including a 6, and he may again find himself leaving a direct shot.

111

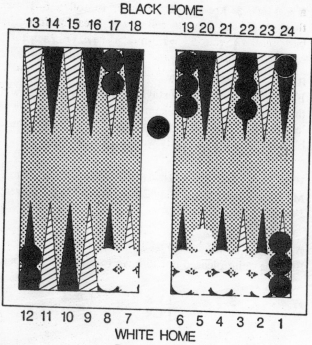

Diagram 8.21

There is, however, a way to play this 5–3 that won't expose white to dangers.

RULE: When your opponent owns your 1 point, and you have a 6 point prime extending from your 2 point to your 8 point, you should, when finally forced to bring men in from either your 7 (bar) point or your 8 point, do so from the bar point. Now, if you roll an embarrassing number such as 6–5 or 6–4, you can play it without leaving a direct shot. If you roll a 6–1, you may have to leave a blot on 8, but it will be exposed only to a 6–1. There are only 2/36 ways to roll a 6–1, but there are 11/36 ways to roll any 6. Breaking from the bar point is therefore 5½ times as safe. Furthermore, if your opponent has a man on the bar, there will be no numbers for him that will hit your blot on point 8. 6–1, which might hit for him if he weren't on the bar, must now be used to come in.

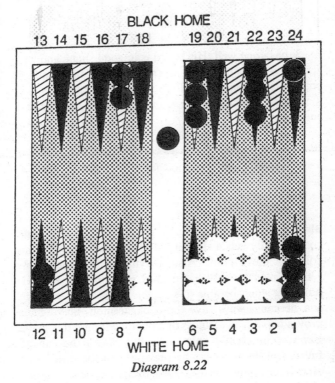

BLACK HOME

WHITE HOME

Diagram 8.22

You also get the added bonus of 6–6 becoming an excellent roll, rather than a completely wasted one.

B	4–2	∅	
W	5–3	8–5	8–3
B	6–1	B–1–7	
W	6–4	6–0	6–2
B	3–3	17–20	12–15–18
		17–20	

Black has done well. His board is in good shape and will get better before it gets worse. Notice what kind of board black would have if he had had to play the 6–6 that he rolled awhile ago when he was on the bar and couldn't move.

W	6–4	5–0	4–0

This is not looking too good for white. 6–6, 5–5, 6–4, 5–4, all leave shots.

B	6–5	7–13	12–17

Black shouldn't run the back checker. If he does, and he eventually gets a shot, it will be at the expense of his point on the 1 point. Also, playing as has been done gets the men forward where they may prove useful. He probably won't be able to save the gammon by running, and he can always save the backgammon. Staying improves his overall chances of actually winning this game. But . . . he should only make this play if he can get full use of the numbers by playing with the other men. And if he thinks he can save the gammon, he should run for sure!

W	5–2	5–0	5–3
B	4–1	17–21	13–14
W	6–4	4–0	4–0

Black has a shot.

B	5–2	1–6	19–21

This is the time to get off the 1 point. There are slight chances of saving the gammon, and it's time to consider that possibility. Also, only doubles by white will leave a shot on this roll.

W	4–2	4–0	2–0
B	4–1	6–7	14–18
W	3–3	3–0	
		3–0	
		3–0	
		3–0	

B	3–1	1–4	22–23

This move produces the position in Diagram 8.23 that follows. White must leave a blot unless he rolls doubles. If white rolls any 1, he will have to leave a double shot. 22–23 is played in anticipation of hitting a blot. Black is hoping the following things will happen:

1. White rolls a 1. If white rolls any number with a 1 (except 1–1), he will be able to bear only 1 man off, leaving two blots still in play.

2. Black hopes to hit one of these blots. Otherwise, the game is over.

3. If black hits a blot, white will eventually come in and in doing so will hit a black blot.

4. Black now hopes that his man on the bar will be able to hit the other white blot, sending two men back. If all this comes to pass, black will have excellent chances to win the game.

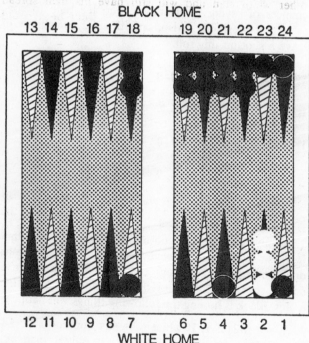

BLACK HOME

13 14 15 16 17 18   19 20 21 22 23 24

12 11 10 9 8 7   6 5 4 3 2 1

WHITE HOME

Diagram 8.23

W   4–1   2–0   2–1X

This is what black hoped for.

B   6-2   **B–2X**   7-13

Black got his man which was a slight hope. 7-13 is played on the theory that it's important to get a man into play as quickly as possible. He shouldn't play 18-24. In this position, he can't win unless he can capture that second man. Black *wants* white to come in as soon as possible. Now black will get a shot at the other white man and will still have his men spread around the board ready to attack the white blot should it manage to escape from black's board.

W   1-1   **B–24X-23X**   Ø

B   6-4   **B–6**   **B–4**

W   5-2   **0**

Can't play.

B   3-1   13-16-17

Black, if he gets hit on point 17, will now be able to aim at white's blot on 1. Being hit will also send the man on 17 back where it will do some good—it may be able to hit white's other blot.

W   6-4   23-17X-13

B   4-1   **B–1X**   4-8

W   6-5   Ø

B   2-2   1-3-5-7   6-8

117

W	4–1	B–24	13–9
B	5–1	8–9X–14	
W	4–4	Ø	
B	5–4	8–12–17	
W	3–2	B–23	Ø

Look at Diagram 8.24. Black has a 3.2 to take. How should he play it?

BLACK HOME

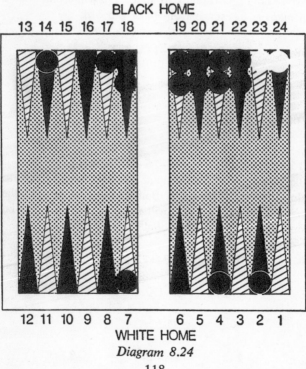

Diagram 8.24

B   **3–2**   **14–17–19**

This is a rather unusual position. One's first instinct is to play 14–17, which makes a prime, and play the 2 with one of the other men. This play, however, is one of the very first times when the normal move of making a prime is wrong. If black does play 14–17 6–8, for example, he will have his prime, but it won't be enough for him to win. Eventually, some position like that in Diagram 8.25 will be reached. Now, if not already, white

BLACK HOME

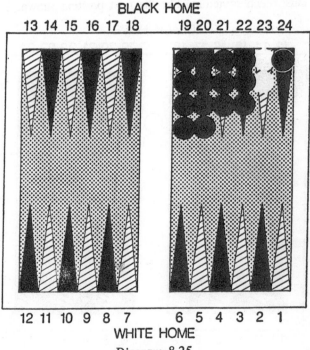

Diagram 8.25

may be able to escape, and black will surely lose. White

119

has been able to get away before black has taken any men off. Long experience has shown that when the opponent has taken thirteen men off, as in the case here, one cannot win unless he gets six or seven of his own men off while both of his opponent's men are either on the bar or, at worst, still in the home board. In this position, no checkers have been taken off, and white is ready to escape. Black can get lucky, but he is an underdog. In order for black to win this game, he must reach something like the next position shown. If

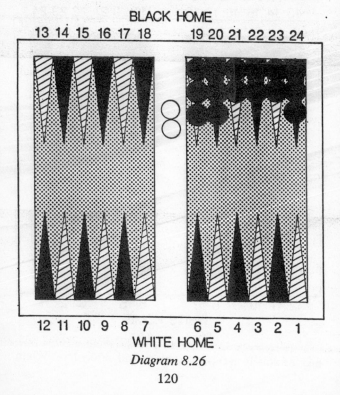

Diagram 8.26

this situation can be achieved, black will be almost even win. It is far far better for him to risk his small chances of winning, to try for this position.

If black can get five men off before white comes in with either man, black can double. Black must not make the prime at this time. Instead, black plays 3–2   14–17–19. Now, when white eventually rolls a 6, he will have to play 23–17X. Black specifically left a blot on point 17 so that when it is hit, it can go back. He will then have four men with which to catch the white blot. One more reason for giving white the shot now is that if white rolls 6–6, he can escape with only one man. If black waits too long to give the shot, white may be able to make the 23 (2) point. If that happens, 6–6 will make white an automatic winner since he will be able to run safely with *both* men.

W	6–3	23–17X–14

B	5–4	B–5	2–6

Black shouldn't hit now on point 24. It would burn a man unnecessarily.

W	3–1	24–23	14–11

White must play 24–23 in the hopes of escaping, unlikely though it may be.

B	5–1	6–11X–12

W	4–3	0

B	6–2	12–18–20

This man is a builder, hopefully towards making the 23 (2) point.

W	6–5	Ø	

B	6–6	5–11–17–23X	7–13

Black shouldn't play 18–24. He wants his men in front
18–24
of the white ones, not behind them.

W	5–1	B–24	Ø

B	4–4	20–24X	19–23
	13–17–21		

W	1–1	B–24X	Ø
		B–24	

This roll is not quite as good for white as it looks. Black
is going to have to let white out again and then chase
after the blot in an effort to recapture it. Black's position is good because he has been able to keep quite a
few men back to engage in headhunting. If, however,
after black makes room for white to escape, white can
roll 6–6, white will again be the runaway favorite. In
general, however, this position is fairly routine for
black. It may take awhile, but black should be able to
get the end position he wants. Strangely enough, the roll
that black doesn't want to see white have, 6–6, is the
same roll black does not want for himself! Black needs
time to go through the routine of bagging and returning
the white blots, and consecutive doubles on black's dice
is about the only thing that can ruin black's strategy.
Look what would have happened to black if on his next
roll he shot 6–6 and then followed it with 5–5.

B **6–1** **B–6** **18–19**

This roll lets white out while black has men back to
wait for them. Only the aforementioned 6–6 will be
bad for black if white rolls it. Playing this way gives
the situation in Diagram 8.27. If white hits the blot
on point 18, that man will go back, and black will have
three men to aim at the white escapee.

BLACK HOME

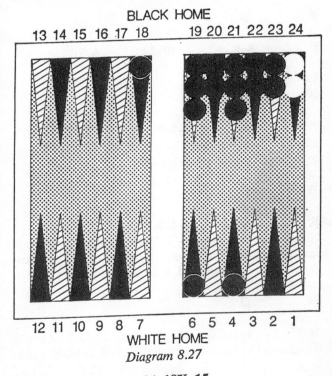

Diagram 8.27

W **6–3** **24–18X–15**

White would much rather not have to hit now. Better

123

for him if he rolled no 6's until black's men were all inside. White, when he does escape, does not wish to be caught. If black's men on points 4, 6, and 18 were on 19, 20, and 21 instead, white's escape would be far more worthwhile. As it is, it's probably for naught.

B	5–3	B–5	21–24X

W	3–2	Ø

B	5–2	19–24	6–8

W	Ø

White can't even roll.

B	2–2	5–7–9	8–10	4–6

Black is literally aiming at white. It will be hard for him to miss. Only 4–4 and 1–1 miss.

W	Ø

B	6–1	9–15X	6–7

Notice that by playing 6–7, black won't leave a blot if he rolls 6–6 twice in a row. This may seem like a small point, but it has happened. It costs nothing to be careful!

W	Ø

B	4–2	15–19	10–12

Continuing to avoid the dangers of 6–6, twice in a row.

W	Ø

124

B	5–4	7–12–16	

W	∅		

B	5–2	12–17	19–21

Black now is concerned with the possibility of rolling just one 6–6.

W	∅		

B	4–4	16–20	17–21–0
			21–0

W	∅		

B	4–2	19–21	19–23

Black is now a tiny favorite.

W	6–2	B–19	∅

It is important for white to come in on this roll.

B	3–3	20–23	21–24	22–0
				22–0
W	2–2	∅		

B	5–2	20–0	23–0

W	2–1	∅	

White could not afford *not* to come in. White would have liked to hit black's blot, but missing it would not have been the end of the world, if he had been able to come in. As it is . . .

| B | Double |
| W | Resign |

This was one of the most interesting games among those considered for this book. If nothing else, it should serve to show that in backgammon, you almost always have a chance. Black was a bit lucky to win, for sure. His play of 4–2 in the middle game was poorly chosen, but he did well to recover. Make note of black's play in the end game. You should particularly understand the reasons behind the plays made in Diagrams 8.24 and 8.27. If you feel so inclined, you might set up a board and play it out ten times.

GAME 10

| B | 6–1 | 12–18 | 17–18 |
| W | 4–2 | 8–4 | 6–4 |

| B | 4–3 | 12–15 | 1–5 |

This play of 1–5 is not usually done, but here it has been selected because black doesn't want to play 12–16 and strip the 12 point.

| W | 4–1 | 6–5X–1X |

This is why black's last play is not usually tried.

| B | 3–2 | B–3 | B–2 |
| W | 4–1 | 6–2X–1 |

126

This may not be best, but it keeps black from using some numbers like 5–1 or 3–1, which would make the 20 (5) point.

| B | 6–2 | B–2 | 12–18 |

Black doesn't play 3–9. If he does, white can hit the 9 blot from point 13. This move both sends black back and brings white's men into play. By staying where he is, black can't be hit to white's advantage, except with an unusual roll.

| W | 6–5 | 13–7–2X |

This is one of those rolls.

| B | 4–1 | Ø |

| W | 6–4 | 8–2 | 13–9 |

| B | 4–4 | Ø |

| White | Double |

| Black | Resign |

Some backgammon games can be fast indeed.

GAME 11

| W | 5–4 | 13–8 | 13–9 |
| B | 6–1 | 12–18 | 17–18 |

W	3–3	8–5	24–21
		8–5	24–21

When the opponent has started to hem one in, 3–3 frequently should be played this way.

B	5–5	12–17–22
		12–17–22

5–5 is often not a pleasant roll. The beginner probably notices this as he plays backgammon.

W	4–2	8–4	6–4

White should give up the 8 point to make the 4 point.

B	6–5	1–7–12

W	3–1	13–10	9–8

B	2–1	19–20–22

W	2–2	6–4–2
		6–4–2

B	6–2	1–3	12–18

Not 1–3–9. White could hit, and black would get only an indirect shot in return. Playing 1–3 doesn't give white many good numbers with which to hit.

W	2–1	10–8–7

This move really puts pressure on black. Black has to get out or else. White's alternative is 10–8 2–1. But this is an invitation for black to run because if he gets hit, he will very likely have a shot in return on the way back in.

B	6–2	3–9–11	
W	4–3	8–5	7–3
B	6–4	11–17	19–23
W	5–4	8–3	5–1
B	6–4	19–23	18–24

Both players do not wish to give a shot. Each hopes the other's board will fall apart first, and in this respect, black has the better game.

W	2–2	13–11–9–7	13–11
B	6–2	12–18	17–19
W	5–4	21–16–12X	
B	3–2	∅	
W	Double		
B	Resign		

Black is happy to get out. White should go for a gammon.

GAME 12

W	5–1	13–8	6–5
B	4–3	1–5X	12–15

| W | 6–2 | B–2 | 24–18 |

When a player is on the bar, 6–2 is one of the worst numbers with which he can come in. This is no exception. The reason this number is so bad is that one almost always comes in with the 2. (One can't come in with a 6). Now the player has to find some useful 6 to take, and this is seldom easy. Sixes are usually better when taken in combination with some other number. Notice also that when one rolls a 6–2 and comes in with the 2, he can't move that man another 6 because the opponent is usually in control of the 8 or 17 (8) point.

B	5–3	17–20	15–20	
W	6–6	13–7 13–7	24–18	8–2
B	6–6	5–11–17–23X 17–23		
W	6–6	∅		
B	6–6	17–23	∅	

This is black's only 6. These 6–6's really happened—with well over 1,000,000 to 1 odds against it. Look what 6–6 twice does to black's position. He still has a man back and his other ones are too far advanced to help that back one. White was actually lucky that he did not have to play his second 6–6.

| W | 6–3 | B–22 | 8–2 | |
| B | 3–3 | 19–22X
19–22 | 1–4 | 12-15 |

W	5–3	0

B	**Double**

Cube from 1 to 2

W	Accept

B	3–3	12–15	19–22
		12–15	
		12–15	

W	6–3	0

White is a small favorite to come in with only two points open. He comes in 20/36 times.

B	6–3	15–21–24

Going for the throat? Not really. It is not quite as aggressive as it looks. There is just no other reasonable way to play. The blot on point 4 can't escape; it's blocked.

W	5–1	B–24X	13–8

B	5–1	B–5	23–24X

Black could have played B-5 4–5, but hitting keeps alive the chances of an easy gammon. If white stays out just once. . .

W	5–1	B–24X	13–8

B	5–2	B–5	22–24X

W	3–1	B–24X–21

This sort of thing can be very annoying to an opponent. Three times in a row white came in and hit as well.

B	4–4	B–4	5–9	15–19
			5–9	

W	2–1	6–5–3

B	5–1	15–20–21X

Black continues to try for the gammon.

W	6–3	∅

B	5–4	4–9–13

W	4–1	B–21X	8–7

White should have played 3–2. The last thing white needs now is a man on the bar.

B	4–2	B–4	19–21X

Still trying.

W	5–4	B–21X	8–3

B	4–3	B–4	13–16

There just isn't any other 3.

W	Double

B	Accept

W	5–1	21–16X–15X

This is one of white's best rolls.

B	5–4	B–5	B–4

Lucky. With two men out on a three point board, black expects to bring both of them in only 9/36 times.

W	4–3	15–12–8	

B	5–5	4–9–14	
		4–9–14	

W	5–3	8–5X	7–2

B	4–2	B–4	9–11

Black shouldn't play 19–21. It breaks up the board. If black gets hit, he will have quite a few return shots.

W	5–3	8–5	8–3

B	4–4	4–8	11–15–19–23

W	5–5	18–13–8X	
		18–13–8	

5–5 can be quite good on occasion. Usually it is best during a running game. Here, though, it brought two men almost home, did safely, and at the same time, it hit a blot. Not bad.

B	6–2	∅	

W	2–1	3–1	2–1

B	5–1	∅	

W	5–5	8–3	7–2
		8–3	7–2

B   5–4   B–4   14–19

Black is now concerned with not losing a gammon. 14–19 brings a man in with no waste of pips.

W   2–1   6–5–3

White, in the position on Diagram 8.28, has a 2–1 to play. One possibility is as noted. The other way is to take two men off. The trouble with 2–0 1–0 is that white will be subsequently exposed to leaving a blot if he rolls 6–6, 5–5, 4–4, 6–4, 6–5 and 5–4. The actual play exposes to 6–2 only.

BLACK HOME

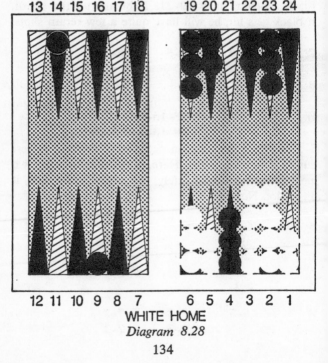

Diagram 8.28

134

B	2–1	9–11–12	
W	6–6	6–0	5–0
		6–0	5–0

If white had not been careful, this roll could have led to an unnecessary disaster.

B	6–6	4–10–16	
		4–10	
		4–10	
W	6–1	3–0	1–0
B	3–3	10–13	12–15
		10–13	
	16–19		

Black wants to get a man off in a hurry to avoid a gammon. Notice black didn't play 15–18–21. This move "wastes" pips and decreases his chances of getting a man off. Efficiency is called for here, and efficient is what black is trying to be with his pips.

W	5–2	3–0	2–0
B	6–4	13–19	15–19

Black is lucky. Two men come in with no waste.

W	5–4	3–0	3–0
B	4–3	13–17–20	

In Diagram 8.29, black has a 4–3 to take. Which outside man should he bring in?

As played, black can get a man off on his next roll

135

with 6–6, 6–5, 6–3, 6–2, 5–5, 5–3, 5–2, 3–3, and 2–2—14/36 ways. Playing instead 14–17–21, black can get one off with the 6–6, 6–5, 6–4, 6–3, 6–2, 5–5, 4–4, 3–3, and 2–2—13/36 ways.

BLACK HOME

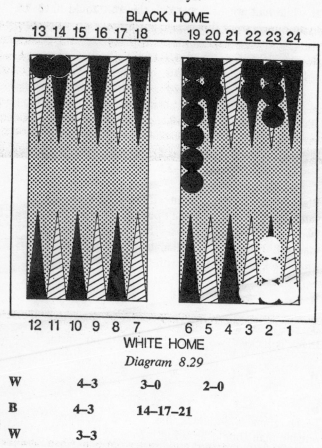

13 14 15 16 17 18   19 20 21 22 23 24

12 11 10 9 8 7   6 5 4 3 2 1

WHITE HOME

Diagram 8.29

W	4–3	3–0	2–0
B	4–3	14–17–21	
W	3–3		

Well, well, well. Backgammon is an easy game.

W	5–1	13–8	6–5	
B	4–4	1–5X	17–21	12–16
			17–21	
W	3–3	B–22	8–5X	13–10
			8–5	
B	5–4	B–4	12–17	
W	3–1	13–10	6–5	
B	4–1	16–20	19–20	
W	3–1	5–4X–1X		

Hitting two men again. If black stays out with one or even both of his men white may have a chance to get something going.

B	3–3	B–3	19–22X	
		B–3	19–22	
W	6–3	Ø		
B	Double			
W	Resign			

Black would have doubled regardless of what white rolled. And white would have to pass.

GAME 14

W	4–1	13–9	6–5

B	3–1	1–4–5X	

As always. Just like Game 9. When the opponent slots a blot on the 5 point, one should hit it whenever possible, 1–1 being the exception.

W	2–2	B–23	13–11–9
	24–22		

Splitting from point 24 to point 22 is not a good thing to do in general. It's better to make a split like 24 to 23. Black won't normally hit white on 23, but when white moves out to 22, he allows black to hit him with 5–3 and 5–5, which makes these rolls much better for black than normal. On the other hand, white has good chances to make black's bar point.

B	5–4	5–10–14

The other obvious play is 1–5 12–17. White, though, is threatening to make the 18, 20, or 22 points. Black has played 5–10–14 in order to improve his chances of building his bar or his 20 (5) point.

W	4–4	22–18–14X	9–5
			9–5

138

B	3–3	B–3	12–15
			12–15
			12–15

The normal play of 17–20 leaves a direct shot, since
17–20
white has split his back men.

| W | 3–2 | 24–21 | 23–21 |

White can play 13–11 14–11, but his back men are
in danger of getting trapped. Making the 21 point gives
him a strong back position. He won't mind getting hit
now as much as he would if he did not have the 21 (4)
point.

| B | 3–3 | 12–15–18 |
| | | 12–15–18 |

| W | 1–1 | 21–20 | 13–12 | 6–5 |
| | | 21–20 | | |

White has played 13–12 instead of 14–13 to increase
his chances of making the bar or the 9 point. 13–12
also causes black to have second thoughts about playing
a 6 from point 3 to point 9.

| B | 5–3 | 17–22 | 19–22 |

| W | 6–1 | 13–7 | 8–7 |

This leaves the situation in Diagram 8.30.

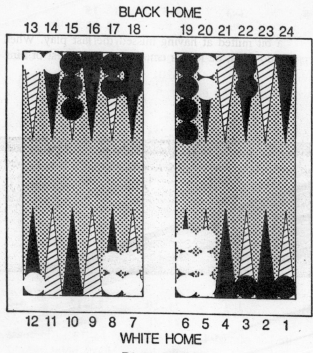

Diagram 8.30

B   6–2   1–3–9

This play is quite wrong. Aside from white's three blots bearing on black's man on point 9, black had a good move available in 15–21 19–21. When the game was actually played, the player admitted that he had overlooked the right play.

W   **Double**

Cube from 1 to 2.

B   **Accept**

Black should not accept this double. At the time, black was a bit miffed at having missed the last play. When white doubled, he let his emotions get the best of him.

As you play, you will probably find yourself subject to a wide range of feelings. For instance, you stay on the bar for four consecutive rolls when the opponent had only a two or three point board, or perhaps your opponent just rolled a 6–1, which was the only number to keep you from winning the game. There is a lot of psychology in backgammon, and if you can manage to control your temper while everyone else is losing theirs, you can do quite well.

W   **6–2**   **14–12**   **13–7**

It was hard to miss! Actually, it might be right for white to hit black on the 3 point. The only trouble with this play is that black may be able to pick up one or more of those blots that white has on his outer board.

B   **6–4**   **3–9**   **19–23**

Black keeps the extra man on point 15 in order to handle 6's.

W   **6–3**   **8–2**   **5–2**

When white missed that blot, the game changed. Black is slightly ahead in the race and has a good position.

B   **6–2**   **15–21–23**

No need to run from point 9. Too dangerous. If black had left a blot on 9, white would have 16/36 ways of

141

hitting. If black had left the blot on 11, white would have 15/36 ways to hit.

W   **4–4**   **20–16–12**
                        20–16–12

There are no real options other than running. At this point, after taking the 4–4, white is 1 pip ahead. Not running would leave the position in Diagram 8.31.

BLACK HOME

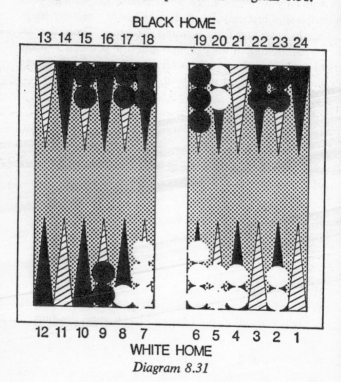

Diagram 8.31

It can be very difficult for white to get out of this position. Why look for trouble when you have at least an even game by running? On the other hand, if the position were as in Diagram 8.32, then white should wait and hope for a shot. The running game is hopeless, and getting a shot is white's best chance to win. Black should not attempt this play if it can cause him to lose a gammon as opposed to losing the game outright.

BLACK HOME

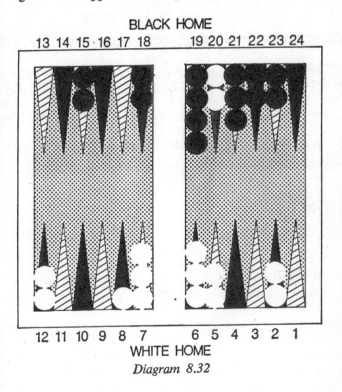

Diagram 8.32

B	6–1	15–21	18–19
W	3–2	7–5	7–4
B	6–5	9–14	9–15
W	4–3	12–9	8–4
B	6–3	14–20	17–20
W	4–4	12–8	8–4
		12–8	
		12–8	
B	6–3	15–21	17–20
W	5–2	8–6	8–3
B	6–1	15–21	18–19
W	3–1	9–6	7–6
B	2–2	23–0	21–23–0
		23–0	

In a bear off position, it is almost always right to take off a man if possible. Here it is right to play 21–23–0 instead of 21–23.

23–23

| W | 4–3 | 4–0 | 3–0 |
| B | 6–1 | 19–0 | 22–23 |

144

W	5–2	5–0	2–0

B	1–1	21–22–23–24–0

In this position (Diagram 8.33), one takes 21–22–23–24–0 rather than, for instance 22–23–24–0 23–24. As played, this leaves men on as many points as possible to cut down on later misses.

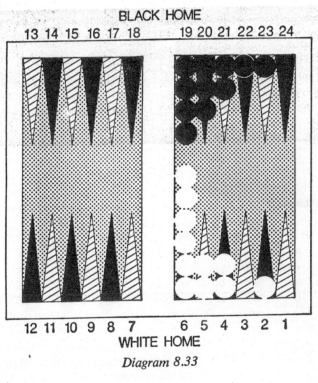

Diagram 8.33

W	4–1	4–0	6–5

B	4–2	21–0	23–0

W	4–2	4–0	2–0

Neither player is rolling particularly well.

B	3–2	22–0	19–21

W	6–5	6–0	5–0

B	3–2	20–22–0	

W	6–4	6–0	6–2

B	6–1	19–0	19–20

W	5–2	5–0	2–0

B	5–4	20–0	21–0

W	4–3	5–1	6–3

Believe it or not, it matters how one plays this number. The objective here is to play to maximize the chances of getting off in two rolls. The choice of plays is 5–1 6–3 or 6–2 6–3. There is a third play of 6–2 5–2, but that is quickly rejected. When trying to get three men off in *two* rolls, one doesn't stack them on the same point if it can be avoided. It turns out that there are 1096 possible combinations of two rolls (36 X 36). Some of these will get both men off on the first roll, that is, double 3's or higher doubles. In all other cases, it turns out that playing as indicated will win out two times more than the alternative play. Rather than working out all the possible combinations at the table (which might bore the opponent to death), one can rely on this general rule. RULE: When there are three men to bear off in two rolls, it is a good policy to put one of them on the 1 point, if in doing so one has not been forced to leave the other two on the same point.

B	3–2	20–22–0	
W	4–2	6–4–0	
B	5–2	20–0	19–21
W	2–1	3–1–0	
B	Double		
W	Resign		

Black shouldn't make the mistake of not doubling. It's easy, when the opponent has just rolled an incredible 2–1 in this position to forget to double. But if he can find a 2–1 on the dice, so can someone else. Double to make him pay for the right to see you do it. White, of course, can't take the double, but he would love it if black forgot to make this double and then rolled 2–1.

GAME 15

B	5–4	12–16	12–17
W	6–1	13–7	8–7

B   **3–2**   **1–3**   **1–4**

This is not the usual way to play 3–2 at all. But, black can't bring two men off of point 12 as he might normally do. It would leave a shot. He might, instead, try 12–14 1–4, but this strips his 12 point of builders and leaves a target for white on his 4 point. Playing as shown, white has two targets. If white hits just one of them, he can hope to come in and cover the one that was not hit. If, on the other hand, white hits both, then black will wish he had tryed the second alternative. 3–2 was a bad roll, and black is not trying to find a good way to play it. Rather, he is trying to find a least bad way to play it.

W   **5–4**   **24–20–15**

B   **4–1**   **3–4**   **12–16**

Black could play 16–20   17–20, making the important 20 (5) point. With white, however, in possession of the bar point, it is a good idea to get the 4 point while it's available.

W   **6–4**   **15–9**   **13–9**

B   **3–1**   **17–20**   **19–20**

W   **6–3**   **24–18–15**

B   **6–1**   **16–22**   **19–20**

Black has played 16–22 instead of 17–23, even though it broke a point, in order to start the 22 (3) point. At this time, it is much better to have the 22 (3) point than the 23 (2) point. Of course, if white had a blot on point 21, then black could not do this. Black probably

148

should have played 17–18, starting his bar point, rather than 19-20.

W	2–2	15–13–11–9–7	
B	1–1	4–5	20–21–22
		4–5	

Black's play of 4–5 is the obvious one to improve his
4–5
chances of escape. In position in Diagram 8.34, white is only 13 pips ahead.

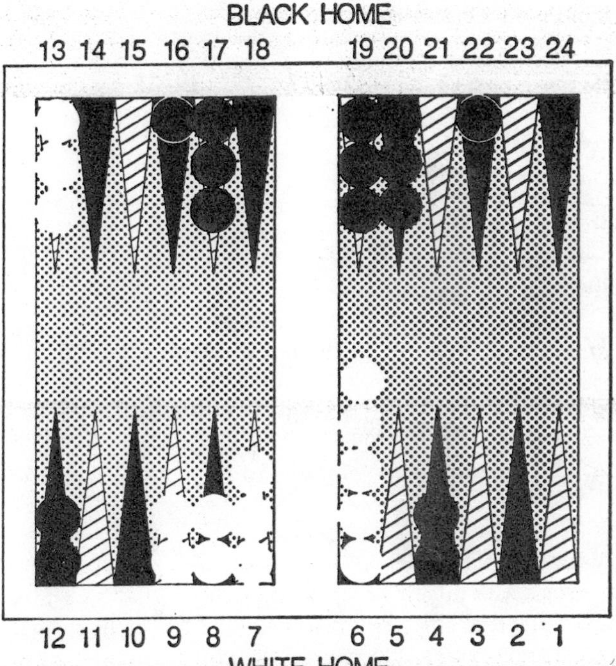

BLACK HOME

Diagram 8.34

On the other hand, there is much to be said for leaving those men on 4 alone. Their presence makes it difficult for white to play 1's and 2's. What, for instance, does white do if he rolls a 6–2? In fact, not moving these pieces may be the better play. This position warranted considerable discussion when it occurred.

W	3–3	13–10	6–3
		13–10	
		13–10	

The 6–3 is played instead of 10–7 or 7–4 to be able to handle 6's on subsequent rolls.

B	5–2	16–21	19–21

W	Double

B	Accept

Clear-cut take. The race now is reasonably even. Count it.

W	6–3	10–4	6–3

B	2–1	12–13	17–19

W	5–3	7–4	6–1

B	4–1	17–18	12–16

W	6–2	10–4	10–8

B	5–1	13–18–19

W	6–2	9–3	9–7

Notice how that point on 5 slows down white's entry.

B	6–3	17–23	18–21

W	6–4	8–2	7–3

B	3–2	19–22	21–23

W	6–2	8–2	8–6

6–6, 5–5, 6–2 will leave a shot.

B	6–5	5–10–16

Black could run with both men, but the race is too much in white's favor. This way, if white rolls one of those numbers listed above, black still gets a shot. Even if black gets hit, there is not much chance of his getting gammoned.

W	5–2	6–1	4–2

White is not able to bring a man in without leaving a shot.

B	4–4	5–9–13–17	16–20

It's almost an even game again. If white had been able to better use his rolls to come in, he would be in a much better position. As it is, black's point on white's board has gained him a lot of time. 4–4 may be just what black needed, short of hitting a white blot, to win.

W	6–2	7–1	7–5

B	4–2	16–20	17–19

W	6–2	6–0	2–0
B	3–3	19–22	22–0
			22–0
			22–0

W	5–2	5–0	2–0
B	5–5	20–0	
		20–0	
		20–0	
		20–0	

W	6–2	6–0	2–0
B	5–4	19–24	21–0

W	2–1	1–0	4–2

White shouldn't play 3–1–0.

B	4–4	19–23	21–0	22–0
		19–23		

W	3–2	3–0	2–0

B	Double

W	Resign

Game 16

B	6–2	12–18–20

152

W	5-4	24-20X-15

Hitting the blot as usual.

B	3-2	B-2	12-15X

W	5-2	B-23	13-8

B	4-1	15-16	12-16

Could hit two men.

W	5-3	8-3	6-3

With 5-3 as an opening roll, white might play 13-8 13-10, although it's close whether he should not make the 3 point. Here, however, it's right to make the point because: 1) Black would have two men bearing on white's blot on point 10, if white put him there, and 2) 13-10 13-8 strips white's 13 point of builders.

B	2-1	16-18	17-18

W	5-5	13-8-3
		13-8-3

As so often happens, 5-5 is not a good roll.

B	Double

Cube from 1 to 2.

W	Accept

This is a somewhat sporty double.

B	6-3	16-22	19-22

W	4-4	8-4	6-2X
		8-4	6-2

153

This may not be best. It burns, or wastes, two men. But it does hit one. Perhaps something good will happen. In the meantime, all of these double numbers are advancing white too quickly.

B   5–3 B–5–8X

W   5–2 B–23   13–8X

B   2–1 B–1   12–14

This is a matter of leaving as few shots as possible.

BLACK HOME

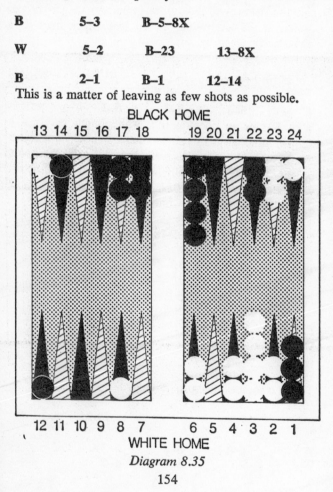

Diagram 8.35

W	6–2	23–21	13–7

In Diagram 8.35 white has a 6–2 to take. In some situations, white might consider trying to make the 5 point, in which case he would play 13–7–5. In this instance, however, it is more important to get the bar point. If the bar point can be had, black may be a long time in getting out.

BLACK HOME

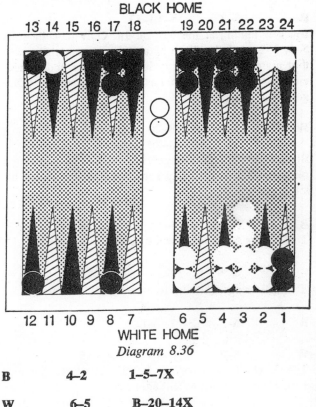

Diagram 8.36

B	4–2	1–5–7X
W	6–5	B–20–14X

155

B	5–1	B–5	7–8X

W	6–3	∅

B	1–1	19–20–21X
		19–20–21

W	4–3	∅

B	5–3	5–10–13

Black is aiming at the blot on 14. Only if white rolls 5–5, 2–2, or 1–1 will he be able to do something with that man. Look at the freedom black has under these circumstances when white has two men on the bar (Diagram 8.36).

W	5–5	B–20	14–9–4
		B–20	

Black's target has disappeared. When this game was played, black looked like someone had just stolen his lollipop.

B	6–1	8–14	13–14

This blocks 6–6 should white roll in.

W	4–3	23–20	24–20

This roll brings white up to even money or better.

B	6–5	1–7–12

W	5–3	4–1X	20–15

The 3 was almost forced, but it does have the nice added bonus of hitting a man.

B	6–2	∅	
W	4–2	3–1	20–16
B	6–6	∅	
W	3–1	16–13	3–2
B	5–3	B–5	12–15X
W	2–1	B–23	13–12X
B	4–2	∅	
W	6–3	23–20	12–6
B	6–3	∅	
W	**Double**		
B	**Accept**		

Black ought to pass this one.

W	6–3	6–3	∅

White has only a 3 to play. He has no 6.

B	2–1	∅	
W	5–2	20–15X–13	
B	3–1	∅	
W	4–3	20–16–13	

B   4–3   Ø

W   5–2   20–15–13

White might have played here 20–15 13–11, thus attacking the 5 point. (See Diagram 8.37) But white has such a lock in this game, it would be silly to lose it if black rolled 5–5, coming in with both men and hitting on 15 as well. White decided to play 100% safe.

BLACK HOME

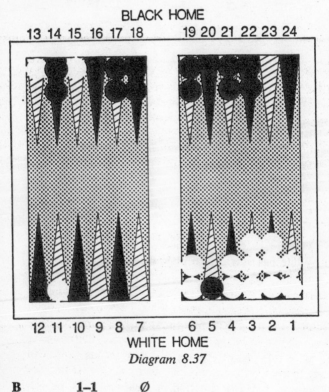

Diagram 8.37

B   1–1   Ø

158

W	5-1	13-12	13-8

B	6-4	∅

W	4-2	12-8-6

Not 13-9-7, which would leave a blot if white next rolled 6-6.

B	3-2	∅

Black would like to come in and get that 5 point.

W	6-4	13-7	8-4

B	3-1	∅

W	5-3	7-4	6-1

This play leads to the situation in Diagram 8.38. This position leaves a shot if white next rolls a 6-1 or a 5-1, a total of 4 rolls.

White could, if he wanted, play 7-2 3-0, to create the position shown here. Only 6-5, or a total of two rolls, will leave a shot. Which is better?

Here, strangely enough, one should prefer the position that leaves twice as many shots as the other. Strange? Yes, for sure. Here is the reason. If one makes the move shown in Diagram 8.39, he will, eventually, unless he roll doubles first, have to move into the position shown in Diagram 8.38. It is better, therefore, to go there right away. Playing this way means white will have to contend with only one bad position. If he goes right away into the situation in Diagram 8.39, he will

13 14 15 16 17 18   19 20 21 22 23 24

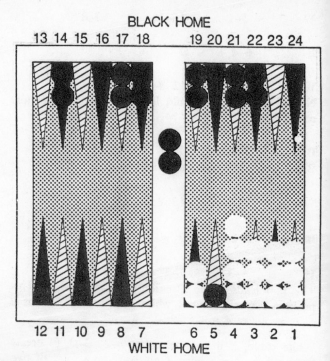

12 11 10 9 8 7   6 5 4 3 2 1

WHITE HOME

Diagram 8.38

eventually roll something like 6–2, 5–3, etc. and he will play it by moving one man off the 6 point and probably one man off the board. And what does he have left? He has the position in Diagram 8.38 and all its problems. He may of course, be able to get the two checkers off the 6 point with no mishap. But had he started this end position (Diagram 8.38) in the first place, that number he rolled to get him out of the later (Diagram 8.39) and into the former (Diagram 8.38) would also have gotten him out of the former (Diagram 8.38) and out of trouble.

160

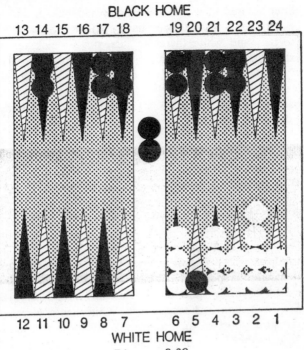

BLACK HOME

13 14 15 16 17 18   19 20 21 22 23 24

12 11 10 9 8 7   6 5 4 3 2 1

WHITE HOME

Diagram 8.39

One more reason for the former position. If white should give a shot that gets hit, he will be giving it earlier than if he had played the latter move. Black will likely still have a man on the bar after hitting him and this situation may give white some extra time to get back in and on the way home.

B	4–3	Ø	
W	5–1	6–1	6–5X

White doesn't have to hit. In this position, he is just

about assured of a gammon and would like to do his best to get it. Black does have two men already on the bar, and white therefore hits, not to pick up an extra man, but to gain some time. If black hits back, white may be able to get back in and, hopefully, get around the board before black gets the rest of his men back into play. This is the reason why white played the roll before as he did.

B	4–3	∅	
W	6–5	5–0	4–0
B	6–3	B–6	∅
W	5–1	4–0	3–2

White doesn't take two men off because it would leave a dangerous position. Taking two off by 5–0 1–0 would leave the situation in Diagram 8.40. Now 6–6, 5–5, 4–4, and 3–3 leave shots. White has a gammon for sure, short of an accident. White now is rooting hard for black to come in. Once black is in, white will have no further worries.

B	5–2	B–5	∅
W	3–2	4–1	4–2

Again, no men off. Safety first!

B	3–3	∅	
W	6–6	3–0	2–0
		3–0	2–0

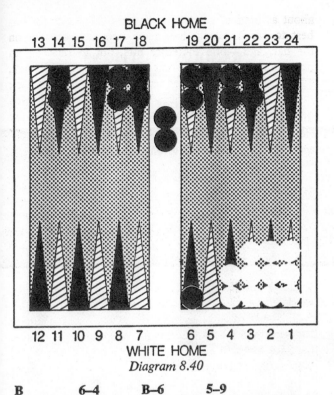

BLACK HOME

13 14 15 16 17 18   19 20 21 22 23 24

12 11 10 9 8 7   6 5 4 3 2 1

WHITE HOME
Diagram 8.40

B   6–4   **B–6**   5–9

Black did not want to come in. There was a chance for a shot if white had not rolled an ace on his next roll. But black is in, and it's all over.

W   5–5   2–0   1–0
                           2–0
                           2–0

B   **Concedes the gammon**

163

9

RANDOM POSITIONS

This section is comprised of a number of positions that represent some common situations. A few of them came up in the play section and are included here for a deeper look than was given them before. Others are

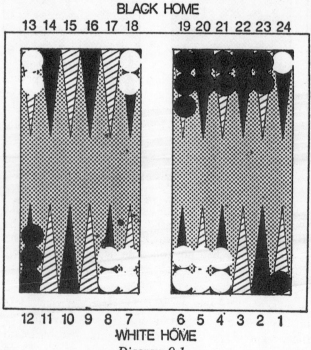

Diagram 9.1

positions of interest that, if studied and understood, can help with one's overall concept of backgammon.

Backgammon is a very versatile game and new and different problems continue to appear. No number of games in the play section could ever contain every possible position or demonstrate every concept. As one plays, he will discover many unusual problems, whose solutions come only from experience. It is hoped that at the end of this book, the reader will be well on his way to acquiring that experience.

In Diagram 9.1, black is faced with the problem of getting his man on white's 1 point to safety. To do this, he must get to the 3 point first and then roll a 6. If black rolls a 1 now, he should *not* use it to come to the 2 point. That play would leave only 1's to permit the blot to get to the 3 point later. There are 11 chances out of 36 of rolling a 1 on any roll of the dice. If black stays on the 1 point, he can then get to the 3 point with any 2 *plus* 1–1. This makes 12 chances out of 36.

In Diagram 9.2 white rolls 5–2. White can point on black on the 1 point, but should he? The alternative play is 7–2, leaving a blot, and 6–4.

Look at the problem this way. Black, if white hits him, will need a 2, followed by a 6, to escape. If he doesn't hit him, he will need a 1, followed by a 6 to escape. Both combinations are equally likely. If, however, black doesn't roll these numbers, he will have to break up his board. So, if white doesn't hit him and he rolls bad numbers, he loses his board. If white does hit him and he doesn't come in, he won't have to play those numbers. As long as black is on the bar, his board remains intact. Look what double 4's or 3's do to

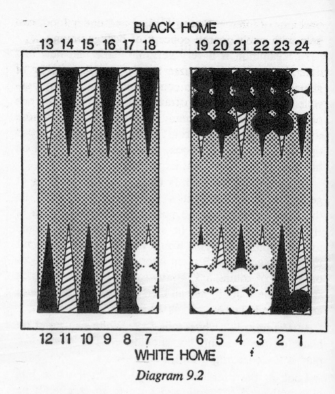

Diagram 9.2

black's game. If he is not on the bar, he will have to play these numbers, and he won't like it at all. Even some simple rolls like 4–3, followed by 3–2 will be excruciating for black as long as he is not on the bar.

In 9–3 white rolls a 5–1, comes to the 8 point with the 5. This 1 should be played from the 6 point to the 5 point. Now numbers like 4–1 and 2–1 make the 4 point,

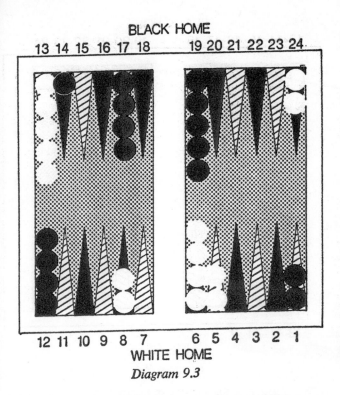

Diagram 9.3

which they did not do before. It is a good idea to keep builders on as many points as possible.

In Diagram 9.4, white rolls a 3–1. Normally, when the opponent has left a blot on his 5 point, one should hit it rather than make his own 5 point. Here though, white has already got three black men back. With this slight advantage, it is better to take his own 5 point.

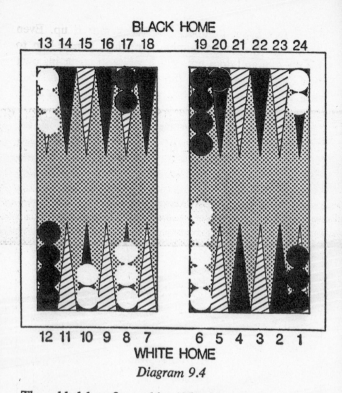

13 14 15 16 17 18   19 20 21 22 23 24

12 11 10 9 8 7   6 5 4 3 2 1

WHITE HOME

Diagram 9.4

The added benefits to him if he hit a fourth man are not as great as they were when he hit the third.

Diagram 9.5 is from Game 4. Black has a 4 to play. In the play section, it was suggested that 7–11 was correct since it cut down on the number of rolls that hit. Further analysis indicates that there is a lot to be said for staying on 7 and playing 13–17 instead. Now 6–2, 6–3, and 6–4 leave a shot that would not have been available had black moved up. 2–1 and 1–1 become bad numbers for white whereas they would have been super numbers had black moved up. Even 5–5, a great running number for white, forces him to hit the blot and does not permit white to cover his own blot on the 1 point. On the other hand, 5–1 and 5–2 now become very fine rolls for white since they both hit the blot and cover the 1 point.

On balance, it appears that the best play is 13–17, not 7–11 as was done in the play section. The position is worth examining in terms of each possible roll and how it would be played in each position, that is, the black blot on 11 versus the black blot on 7.

BLACK HOME

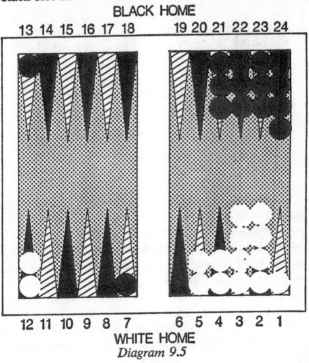

Diagram 9.5

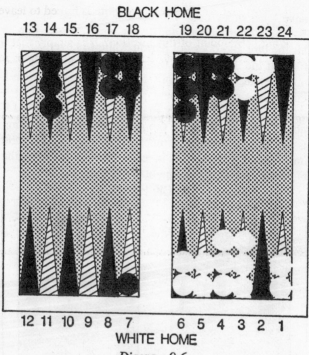

Diagram 9.6

In Diagram 9.6 white has a 2 to play. One's first instinct is to play 4–2, but doing this will force him to play subsequent 5's from 6 to 1. If he plays 6–4 instead, he will be able to keep his men alive. This play gives up the 6 point but gives the player a chance to keep some semblance of a board.

In Diagram 9.7 white is probably going to win the game, and possibly a gammon. The only way he can lose is if he gets hit during the bearing off. Black, with four men on the bar, has quite a bit of time. He may still have a man on the bar when white is forced to leave a shot.

What is the point of this position? It is simply that it is not always necessary to hit everything in sight once a player has achieved a closed board. Black has a blot on point 12. It is possible that white might have hit it. White, if he had had the opportunity, has done well not to hit it.

Normally, only one or two opponent's pieces are trap-

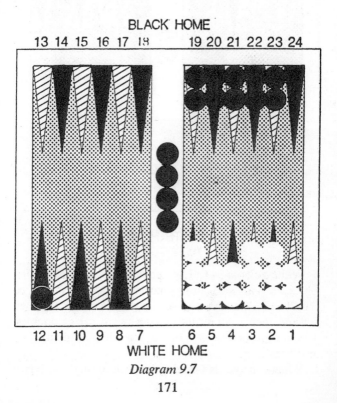

Diagram 9.7

ped like this, and once they come in, the bear off can continue in peace. These extra black men are not as much of an asset to white as one might think.

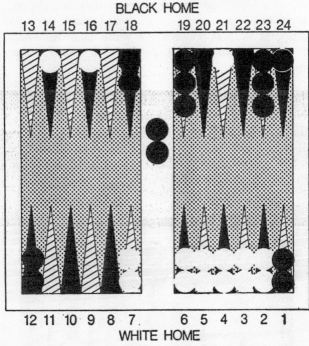

BLACK HOME

13 14 15 16 17 18   19 20 21 22 23 24

12 11 10 9 8 7   6 5 4 3 2 1

WHITE HOME

Diagram 9.8

White rolls a 3–1. How should he play? Note that black has two men on the bar. White's play should be 21–20–17. The thing to avoid here is piling the men up and then running into an awkward set of doubles. If white plays 16–13   14–13, he will find double 1's will break up his prime.

When a player is bringing his men around the board

and he isn't concerned with being hit, he should try to avoid placing his outside men on the same point. He may have later reason to regret it.

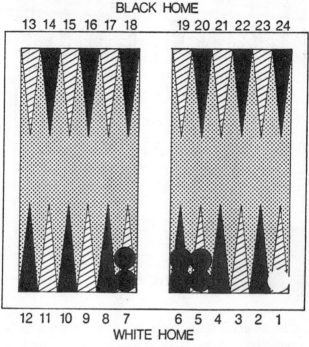

BLACK HOME

13 14 15 16 17 18   19 20 21 22 23 24

12 11 10 9 8 7   6 5 4 3 2 1

WHITE HOME

Diagram 9.9

Diagrams 9.9 and 9.10 are included as a pair to show the difference between the effectiveness of three blocking points as opposed to four blocking points.

Diagram 9.9 provides black with the following escape numbers: 6–1, 6–2, 6–3, 5–2, 5–3, 4–3. There are, therefore, twelve combinations that allow black to escape.

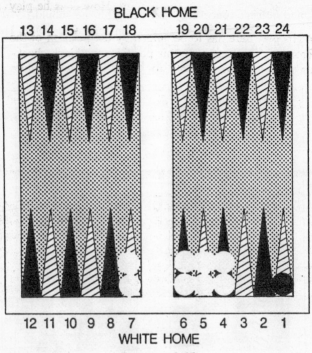

BLACK HOME

13 14 15 16 17 18   19 20 21 22 23 24

12 11 10 9 8 7   6 5 4 3 2 1

WHITE HOME

Diagram 9.10

In Diagram 9.10, white has a fourth point in his prime. This restricts black to the following escape numbers: 6–1, 6–2, and 5–2. This is six combinations or exactly half of the combinations available to escape for black when he had only three points.

The strength of this position will be more appreciated when the reader becomes involved in doubling or accepting doubles.

Diagram 9.11 is a bear off position. White rolls 6–1

174

and takes a checker off the 6 point. How does he play this 1?

His play here has to be guided by the position of the remaining black men. In this position, the black checkers will be off in two rolls for sure. This means white will get only one more roll, if he gets that. Therefore white must play his 1 in order to maximize his chances of getting off in one roll. This can be done by playing 4–3. Now the three men can be taken off with 6–6, 5–5,

BLACK HOME

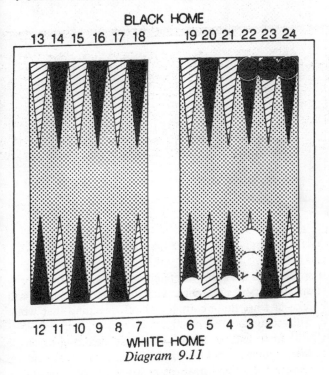

Diagram 9.11

4–4, or 3–3. If it were played 3–2, then double 3's would not take all the men off.

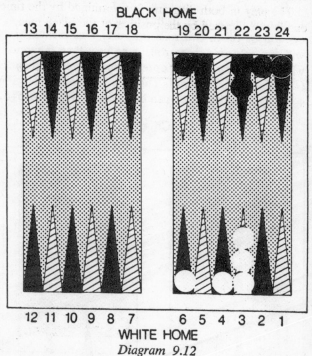

BLACK HOME

13 14 15 16 17 18   19 20 21 22 23 24

12 11 10 9 8 7   6 5 4 3 2 1

WHITE HOME
Diagram 9.12

Diagram 9.12 may seem similar to 9.11, but there is an important difference. Barring doubles, black will take at least three rolls to get off, meaning that white will get to roll twice.

If white rolls 6–1 here, he should bear a checker off the 6 point as before, but this time the 1 should be played 3–2. This move cuts down on the chances of white's getting off in one roll, but it increases the chances of getting off in two rolls.

The play in both diagrams is determined by the time one has as dictated by the position of the black men.

BLACK HOME

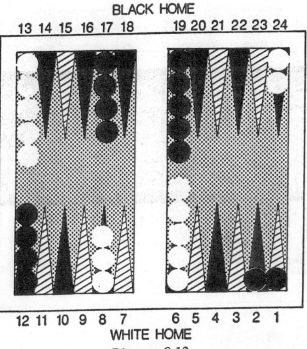

13 14 15 16 17 18   19 20 21 22 23 24

12 11 10 9 8 7   6 5 4 3 2 1

WHITE HOME

Diagram 9.13

White's first roll after black has played is a 4–1. Black has unfortunately split his back men, meaning white can no longer play 13–9   6–5 as he might usually. 13–9 may still be good, but 6–5 is certainly not. Black will have two men aiming at white's blot, which

177

makes the play just too dangerous. Instead, the alternative move of splitting the black men 24–23 is selected. This is merely an example of changing normal strategy according to one's opponent's actions.

BLACK HOME

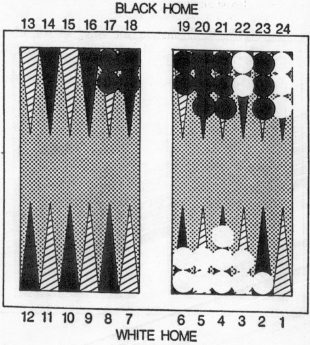

WHITE HOME
Diagram 9.14

In Diagram 9.14, white still has a 2 to take. It looks like 4–2; making a 5 point prime is right, but there is a trap here. What if white rolls a 6 on his next roll? That 6 must be played 22–16, leaving a vulnerable blot on 22 and ruining white's back game as well.

White's correct play is 24–22, thus ensuring that

178

when the 6 is eventually rolled, it can be played safely.

In 9.15 white rolls a 6–4. It is possible for him to keep both men on the 24 point, but that would lead to a backgammon almost any time white doesn't hit a blot.

On the other hand, white can run with both men, getting off the backgammon for sure, except when black rolls double 6's, 5's, 4's, 3's, or 2's. But if white runs with both back men, he will surely be gammoned. Instead, white should run with one back man.

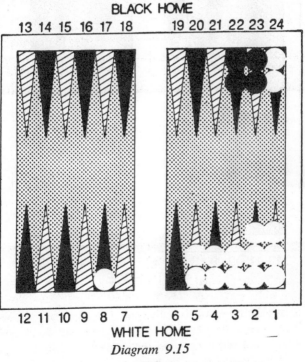

BLACK HOME

13 14 15 16 17 18   19 20 21 22 23 24

12 11 10 9 8 7   6 5 4 3 2 1

WHITE HOME

Diagram 9.15

This move will cost white a backgammon only if he subsequently rolls a number totaling 5 or less pips and does not hit a black blot and if black can get off in two rolls.

Against this, white still has the reasonable chance of hitting a blot and even, though rarely, winning the game.

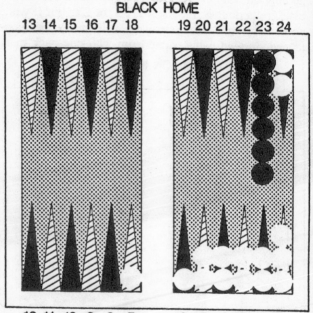

BLACK HOME

13 14 15 16 17 18   19 20 21 22 23 24

12 11 10 9 8 7   6 5 4 3 2 1

WHITE HOME

Diagram 9.16

Whatever white rolls, he should run with at least one back man. Now if black rolls a 1, he will hit white's blot. Now white can win the game if he hits the blot with a 1 on the way back in.

If, in this position, white rolls double 6's, he should run with both men. Whenever one can do so, he should save the gammon. Here, if white doesn't run with both back men, his play will look like this: 24–18–12–6 7–1. The 7–1 is a waste of 5 pips that could be much better used to start running with the second back man.

BLACK HOME

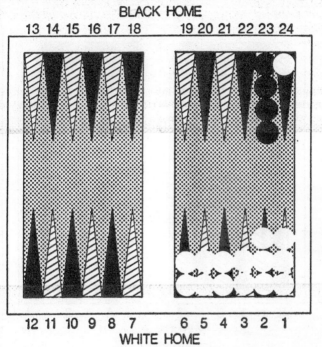

WHITE HOME

Diagram 9.17

White rolls a 4–3. It is best to run in order to try to save the gammon (to say nothing of the backgammon). If black rolls a 1 on either of his next two throws, white will have excellent chances of escaping the gammon.

Waiting on the 24 point is far too risky. After all, if black rolls some number like 4–3, taking off two men, is white going to wait some more? If he now rolls 2–1, 3–1, 4–1, 3–2, or 1–1, he will be backgammoned should black not roll a 1.

BLACK HOME

13 14 15 16 17 18 19 20 21 22 23 24

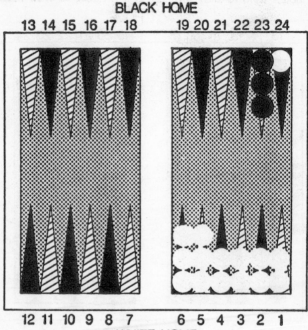

12 11 10 9 8 7 6 5 4 3 2 1

WHITE HOME
Diagram 9.18

Here is the one exception to the rule. Black has three men on the 2 point. Now white should wait, if possible, with that one man, because black will have to leave a shot whenever he doesn't roll doubles. And, if black rolls a 1, white will get a double shot. Suppose black rolls 5–1. He bears a man off and hits white on the 24 point, leaving two blots at which white can aim.

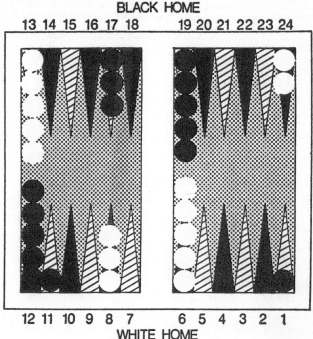

BLACK HOME

13 14 15 16 17 18   19 20 21 22 23 24

12 11 10 9 8 7   6 5 4 3 2 1

WHITE HOME

Diagram 9.19

Black's first roll was 6–4 and he ran a back man. Now, white rolls a 6–4 or a 6–3, and it's his play. No longer can he run with a back man because black will have two men to hit his blot, thus greatly diminishing whatever chance white has of getting away with his normal maneuver. When this happens, one needs an alternate play. This is no bargain, but white should play a man to black's bar point and come down to his 9 or

183

10 point. It will be hard for black to hit the bar point blot without leaving some return shots for white.

BLACK HOME

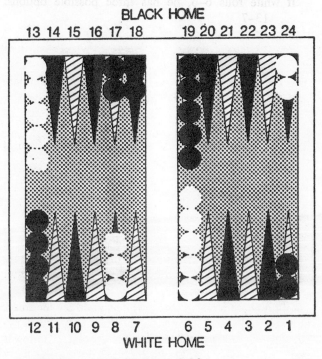

13 14 15 16 17 18   19 20 21 22 23 24

12 11 10 9 8 7   6 5 4 3 2 1
WHITE HOME

Diagram 9.20

Diagram 9.20 was formed when black rolled 6–1, making his bar point. How should white reply with 6–5 or 6–6?

With 6–5, white can play 13–8–2 or 13–8   13–7. White should try the latter on the theory that if his blot on the bar is not hit, he can then make the bar point. Playing 13–8–2 has no particular future. It burns a man for no useful reason. If black doesn't hit the blot, white won't even want to cover it.

If white rolls 6–6, he has three possible options:

    13–7
    13–7
    13–7
    13–7

This leaves a blot on 13 and gives up the very important 13 point. The second play is

    13–7   8–2
    13–7   8–2

This play advances two men to the 2 point, which is of no immediate value.

The third play is

    13–7   8–2
    13–7
    13–7

This play keeps the 13 point intact. The blot on 2 is not too good, but it is a waste of only one man. Being hit there is not too bad for white since it will allow that man to get back into play.

Of the three possible plays, white should try the third, although the first has considerable merit. Avoid, however, the second play of making the 2 point. The fewer men one gets on the 1 and 2 points during the early part of a game, the better it is.

By the way, if black rolls 6–6, making both bar points, and white rolls 6–6 on his turn, white should give up if his opponent will let him.

In Diagram 9.21, white still has a 1 to play. Which 1 should he play? The choices seem to be 17–16, 12–11 or 6–5. One of these is right.

The principle here is known as the "theory of dupli-

185

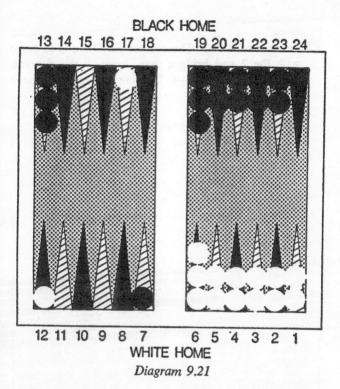

Diagram 9.21

cation." If one has to leave more than one shot, he should try to place his men so that each of them will be hit by the same numbers. If white plays 17–16, he will be hit by any 3 or 5, plus various combinations. If he plays 6–5, he will be hit by any 4 and any 5, plus various combinations. But if he plays 12–11, then *only* 4 will hit him directly, plus the inevitable combinations. But by making the direct shot at both men at the same time, white has significantly increased his chances.

In 9–22 white's opening roll was 4–1, played by

bringing a man to the 9 point and slotting on the 5 point. Black rolled 3–1 and hit the blot on the 5 point. White now rolls 5–2. The correct play here is to come in with the 2 and bring a man down to the 8 point. White shouldn't play 9–4. Leaving the man on the 9 point gives black "duplication." If he rolls a 4, he will be able to either hit white's blot or to make white's 5 point, but not both. If white plays 9–4, a number like 3–1 for black will both hit and cover. If black doesn't roll a 4, white's man on 9 may prove very valuable as a builder.

BLACK HOME

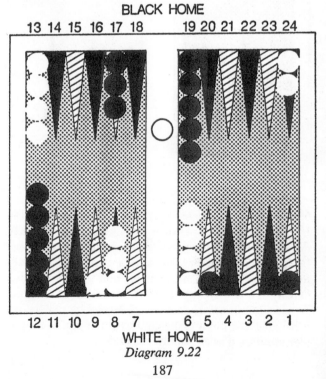

Diagram 9.22

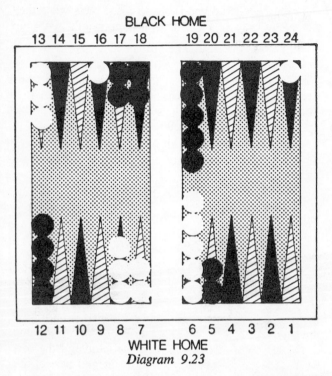

13 14 15 16 17 18 19 20 21 22 23 24

12 11 10 9 8 7 6 5 4 3 2 1

WHITE HOME
Diagram 9.23

White rolls a 4–2. The normal play of making the 4 point should be rejected here in order to play 16–14–10. There are a number of reasons for this move. First, the 4 point loses much value when the opponent has taken the 5 point. Second, it is a good idea to make some effort to save the man on point 16, and third, playing 16–14–10 leaves black a Hobson's choice should he roll a 5. He can either hit the blot at the expense of the 5 point or he can leave the blot there and then see it used as an important builder.

188

Frequently it is a good idea to place blots when they can be hit only as a result of the opponent's giving up a valuable point.

10

THE CUBE—WHEN TO DOUBLE—
WHEN TO TAKE

Mechanics

In backgammon, as in no other game in the world, the participants have the option of increasing the stakes of the game at anytime. This is done through the "cube." All backgammon sets have a die on which is imprinted the numbers 2, 4, 8, 16, 32, and 64. At the beginning of the game, this die is located in the middle of the bar, where, for the moment, it is not an integral part of the game.

At some point during the play, one of the players may decide his position has improved to such an extent that he would like to increase the stakes of the game. He does this by taking the cube, turning it so the 2 is on top, and offers it to his opponent with the phrase, "I double." This has the following effect. The opponent concedes the game and loses 1 point, or the opponent accepts the double and play continues with the stakes of the game now being 2 points rather than the original

1. This doubling is done only by the player whose turn it is to roll and before he rolls the dice.

Once a double has been made, the player who has been doubled now "owns" the cube and he alone has the right to make the next double. Should the dice favor him, he may, at one of his subsequent turns, re-double, which means the stakes go from 2 points to 4 points. The other player has the same options as before. He can accept the double and play for 4 points or he can concede the game and lose 2 points.

Describing the mechanics of the cube is perhaps the easiest thing there is about gammon. But understanding its nuances is surely the most difficult.

Basics

The first thing to understand is that just because one is ahead, he does not necessarily have a double, nor does the fact one is behind mean he must pass a double. It is all a matter of degree. For example, if a player is 55% favorite, should he double? What if he is a 65% favorite? If he has only a 40% chance to win, should he take a double? What should he do if he has only a 30% chance to win?

As it turns out, a player should take most doubles if he has a 25% chance. Here is the logic. If he passes the double, he loses 1 point. That's that—end of game. If he takes the double it means he is playing for 2 points. If he has a 25% chance, he will win one game out of four. This gives him a loss of 6 points for the three games he lost, but it will win him 2 points on the game he wins. This is a net loss of 4 points over the

190

four games or an average loss of 1 point per game. This result is exactly the same if he passed the double in the first place.

Clearly, if it's right to take when a player has only a 25% game, he should take whenever his game is better. The reason is simple. If he passes the double, he loses the amount of the game right away. If he takes the double, he will still lose, but the amount, on the average, will be less than if he passes.

Of course, if a player is in danger of being gammoned, he has to be less inclined to take a double. He can't afford to play in a 25% game if his opponent has any chance to gammon him because the opponent will be able to win twice the amount of the stakes, whereas he can win only the single amount.

Possession of the Cube—Its Value

There's one aspect of the cube that is far too often not understood by the new player, which is "value of possession of the cube." If a player owns the cube, he can do things he would never otherwise have a chance to do. Remember, as long as he owns the cube, he is going to get to finish the game, for he may be able to make a play that will greatly increase his chances of winning. On the other hand, if the opponent holds the cube, one might not be able to make his play because his opponent would double and he wouldn't be able to take it.

Here is an example of what the cube is worth. Let's say a player is given the cube at the start of the game and with it he now has the right to the first double.

What does this do for his chances? As we saw earlier, if one has better than a 75% position, he will be able to double and his opponent will fold. This means that the player has a sure win if he gets from 50% to 75+%. On the other hand, the opponent can't double if he gets to 75% so the player can play the game out. For the opponent to win, he has to achieve a 100% game; his game must go from 50% to 100%. While the prospects of the one holding the cube must go only from 50% to 75+%. Quite a difference. The opponent has twice as far to go. For this reason, once a player has been doubled in a game, and he now owns the cube, he should be less quick to redouble than he would be to make a first double.

Remember this rule: whoever has the cube in what is an even game is a 2 to 1 favorite. The positions most easily judged are running games and bear offs, for the above rule is readily observable. If each player has 100 pips to go in what is an even position, the player with the cube can double if he rolls double 6's and his opponent rolls some nominally small number. This roll will probably cause the other player to resign. Notice that the option to double is not available to the other player, and if he rolls 6–6, he will not be able to end the game by doubling.

Late in the Game

The more play left in the game, the more important the possession of the cube will be. Only as the players near the end of the game and get into one-roll situations will the percentages required for doubles or takes be changed radically.

Normally, these percentages apply when considering whether or not to double. If a player is unlikely to gammon his opponent, and the cube is still in the center of the board (no one has doubled yet), one should double if his chances are about 60%. If he has been doubled and owns the cube and he estimates little chance of getting a gammon, he should redouble when he has about a 66% chance to win. He is, in other words, a 2 to 1 favorite.

If the player feels he may gammon his opponent, he should double a little faster, depending on how strongly he feels about getting a gammon.

One-roll Situations

A one-roll situation is defined as a position where there is going to be exactly one more roll. A typical example might be where a player has two men left to bear off, and his opponent has one man left on his 2 point. Obviously, if the player gets his men off, he wins; if he doesn't, he doesn't. Let's say his men are on his 5 and 2 points. He will get them off in the next roll 19 times out of 36. So he should double, and his opponent should take. Notice that his chances of winning are about 53%. This is not nearly the 60% that was recommended earlier as the number needed for a double. The difference is that in this position, the game is over at the conclusion of his roll. He was not getting another turn.

Similarly, one should double if his two men are on any combination or two points that get taken off more than half the time. If his men are on the 4 and 3 points, his successful rolls number only 17 out of 36. This makes him a slight underdog, and he should not double.

When to Double in a Running Game

When one is in a straight race, he can judge when to double by counting the pips of his men and those of his opponent's and comparing the totals.

If he is leading his opponent by 8% of his total, then he can double if the cube is still in the center of the table.

If he has already been doubled and now owns the cube, he needs at least a 10% lead. The reason he needs more to make a redouble is that ownership of the cube is so important that one does not wish to give it up too easily. Notice the difference between a cube in the middle and a cube that is owned. When it's in the middle, a player does not have the exclusive rights to it that he has when it is on his side.

If one should be doubled by his opponent, he should take it if he is less than 15% of his pip total behind. For example, if the opponent's count is 120, and he doubles, the player should take the double if his count is less than 138—115% of 120.

If the reader doesn't yet fully appreciate the power of the cube, consider this question. Player A and Player B have the following arrangement. Player A gets to start the game with 6–6, making both bar points. Player B gets the next roll and the right to the first double, that is, Player A can't double until Player B has doubled. Who is the favorite? It turns out that Player B has a significant edge.

Here is the logic. If a player gets to start with 6–6,

he will be about a 13–10 favorite to win. In terms of percentages, Player A has a 56% game. Player A, however, does not get to double. For him to win the game, he has to improve his position from 56% to 100%, or a 44% improvement. Player B, on the other hand, has a 44% game, but he has the right to double. He can win the game if he can improve his game to a mere 75+% position because he can then double. Player A should then pass. Player B then has only to improve his game from 44% to 75+%, which is an increase of only 31%. This is significantly less than the 44% improvement required of Player A to win.

Doubles in the Bear-Off Position

When one has reached the bear-off stage, his consideration is no longer so much about the pip count as it is to about the number of remaining rolls.

If it appears that a player is a little bit ahead in the bear-off position, he should double if the cube is still in the middle. On the other hand, if he has already been doubled, he should use the usual caution before redoubling. When he has only 8 men, he should redouble if his men are equal in positions to his opponent's. He should probably pass this double unless he has all his checkers on the 1 and 2 points.

If, in a five-roll position, where both players have ten men, one may redouble if he has a clearly better distribution of his men. If it looks like he will have some misses with his rolls, he should wait for one roll if both he and his opponent have ten men left. In a three-roll position, one should pass if he is doubled. He'll need to roll a useful set of doubles to win, and this occurrance is against the odds. Anyway, his opponent has the same chances of rolling doubles that he does.

Doubles When a Player Has Been Hit After Having Removed Some Men

Every now and then, a player has taken some men off, and he then gets hit and finds himself on the bar against a closed board. How many men does he need to take a double? Is there a situation where he should double his opponent? These interesting questions can be found in the section on doubling positions with an analysis.

Should a player always double when he is far ahead? Usually, he should, but if he is not playing the Jacoby Rule (explained in the next paragraph), he should consider whether or not he might play for the gammon. If he thinks he has good enough chances to gammon his opponent, he should go ahead and try for it, because success will net him 2 units instead of 1. Remember that if one's position is good enough to play for a gammon, his opponent would almost surely pass a double if the player decides to double instead. If the opponent passes, the player can no longer win more than 1 unit (or whatever the value of the cube is at that time).

The Jacoby Rule

Some players, in the interest of speeding up the game, agree that no game where the cube is at the one level may be played for a gammon. Gammons may be played for, and scored, only when the cube is at 2 or higher.

There are variations in this rule, but the idea is good since it avoids long, slow games where not too much is at stake. Decide in advance whether or not to play this rule. I would suggest it in the interests of saving time.

11

CUBE POSITIONS

In this section are a number of positions concerning the cube. Should a double be made and should it be taken? Most of the time the consideration of who owns the cube has been ignored. Its importance is quite significant, but for the time being, the reader should look

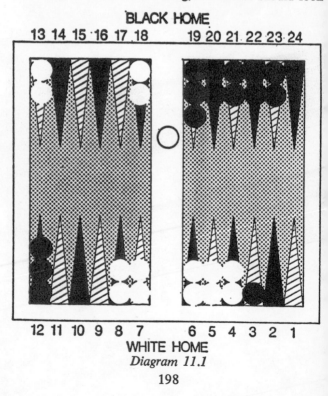

BLACK HOME

13 14 15 16 17 18   19 20 21 22 23 24

12 11 10 9 8 7   6 5 4 3 2 1

WHITE HOME

Diagram 11.1

at the positions, remembering the cube being in the middle. In this section the reader thinks with a player's mind as he evaluates a position, to determine whether to double or take. As the beginner's game improves, he will begin to see how the position of the cube affects the play, and he will make allowances accordingly. To be aware of its importance now will help in the long run to improve overall understanding of the cube.

In Diagram 11.1, black has doubled white. Is the double correct, and if so, should white accept?

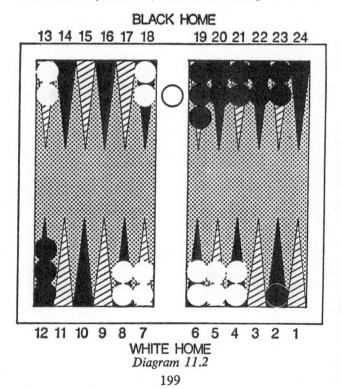

BLACK HOME

Diagram 11.2

Here, as it turns out, black's double should be made and be subsequently rejected by white. Black has too much going for him. A roll with 6's will be used to escape with the back man and most other numbers can be used to bring an extra man into a position to work over the white blot should it be able to come in from the bar. White is in definite danger of being gammoned.

Diagram 11.2 is exactly like 11.1 except that black's blot is on the 2 point, where it needs specifically 6–1 to escape, rather than on the 3 point, where any 6 can

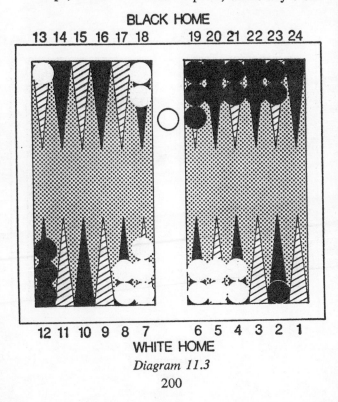

BLACK HOME

13 14 15 16 17 18   19 20 21 22 23 24

12 11 10 9 8 7   6 5 4 3 2 1

WHITE HOME

Diagram 11.3

200

be used for getting out. This difference, slight though it may appear, is so important that black does not have a double. Black's men are advanced to a point where one or two bad numbers will ruin his board while his back man is still a prisoner.

Diagram 11.3 is the same as Diagram 11.2 with one of white's men on point 13 having moved to point 7. This situation affords black the chance to hit another white blot. Strangely enough, though, this is not really worth that much to black. The important thing to notice

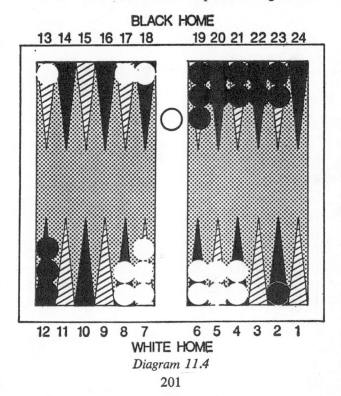

BLACK HOME

13 14 15 16 17 18   19 20 21 22 23 24

12 11 10 9 8 7   6 5 4 3 2 1

WHITE HOME

Diagram 11.4

here is that if black rolls a 1, it is necessary to use it to move from point 2 to point 3. The white blot on point 13 is an illusion, and a tempting one at that. Black is still in danger of having his game fall apart should the blot on point 2 not get away safely.

Diagram 11.4 is the third example again, but with white now having blots on points 13, 17, and 18. Now, in spite of the man still trapped on point 2, black can double, because he can use numbers to hit the blots on points 17 and 18, sending three white men back (count-

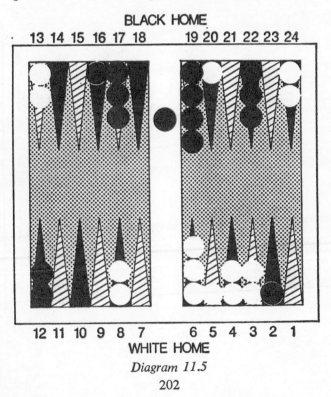

BLACK HOME

13 14 15 16 17 18   19 20 21 22 23 24

12 11 10 9 8 7   6 5 4 3 2 1

WHITE HOME

Diagram 11.5

ing the one already on the bar). The danger to white is now too great for him to take the double. True, black may have to break his board, but even if this happens, white may have to waste too much time trying to come in if he has three, or four, men on the bar. In Diagram 11.5 white doubles and black should pass. Rolls of 1's, 3's, and 8's cover the blot on point 5, making a 4 point prime, while 4's will hit another black blot. White's position is so strong that if he had a man on the bar, instead of black, as in Diagram 11.6, he would still double.

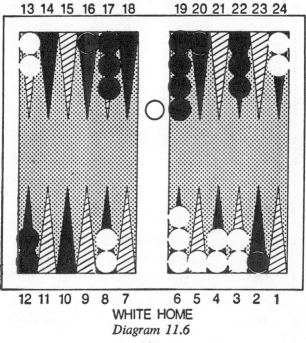

BLACK HOME

13 14 15 16 17 18   19 20 21 22 23 24

12 11 10 9 8 7   6 5 4 3 2 1

WHITE HOME

Diagram 11.6

In this position, 5's will hit, and most 1's and 3's will cover the 5 point. 5–4 hits two men, and 4–4 hits a man and covers the 5 point as well.

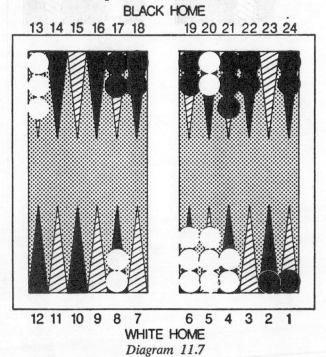

BLACK HOME

13 14 15 16 17 18   19 20 21 22 23 24

12 11 10 9 8 7   6 5 4 3 2 1

WHITE HOME

Diagram 11.7

White doubles and black passes. Black's men are too far advanced to do much good. If his pieces on points 1 and 2 don't get out, it will probably be at the expense of his containing points 17 and 18. As it is, should white run with those men on 20, with for instance a 5–4, black won't have a man available with which to reply.

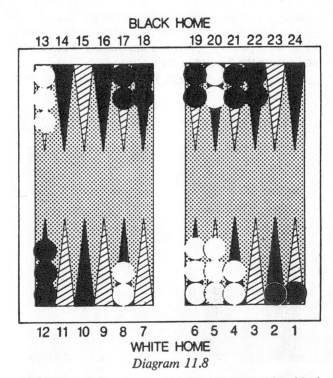

12 11 10 9 8 7   6 5 4 3 2 1
WHITE HOME
Diagram 11.8

Diagram 11.8 is the same as Diagram 11.7 but black has significantly more time available to him now because he no longer has those two men on his 24 point. As a rule, one should try at all costs to avoid making the 1 point (24 point) because it so completely negates the value of these men.

Here, the two men on 24 and the extra one on 21 have been placed on point 12. This situation affords black with significantly more time. Whether it gives black enough time to accept the double is debatable, and it is still probably best to refuse the double. The important thing to recognize here is the value of having those men on point 12, instead of on points 21 and 24. Timing in backgammon is incredibly important, and there can hardly be too many examples of it.

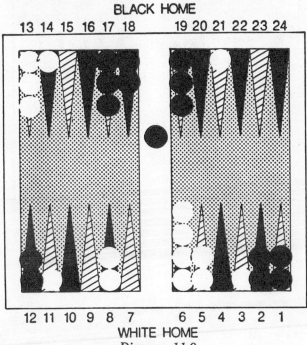

BLACK HOME

13 14 15 16 17 18   19 20 21 22 23 24

12 11 10 9 8 7   6 5 4 3 2 1

WHITE HOME

Diagram 11.9

Even though black owns white's 1 and 2 points, he should pass white's double. The timing is such that white may be able to prime black and then hold the prime long enough to force black to break up his board.

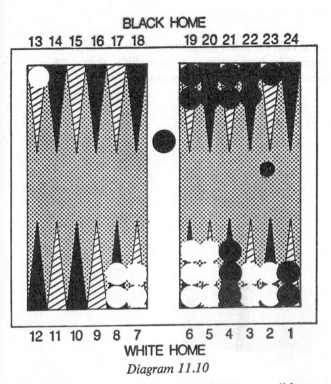

Diagram 11.10

Black has a very marginal take. White may well leave a shot, and black, if he can hit the blot, can easily win the game. The extra men on the bar and 4 point give black enough time to keep the back game alive. If black does hit a man, he can expect to have a good board remaining to contain white's blot. Black should pass the double without those extra men to take up the time slack. It would be better for black if he held white's 1 and 3 points, rather than his 1 and 4 points. The 1 and 4 points are not too effective a back game because white can easily play to the 2 and 3 points, thus getting past black's men on the 4 point. This explains why black should probably pass.

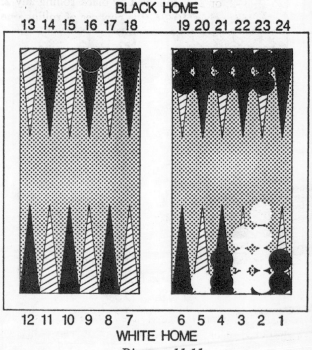

BLACK HOME

13 14 15 16 17 18 19 20 21 22 23 24

12 11 10 9 8 7 6 5 4 3 2 1

WHITE HOME

Diagram 11.11

This position is too good for white to turn the cube. The rolls that are bad for white are 4–4, 4–1, 1–1, and 2–2, or 5 out of 36. Gammon chances are good enough to chance these poor rolls.

Diagram 11.12 shows that the situation is also too good for white to double. White has an excellent shot

208

at a gammon. Only if he rolls a 2, leaving a shot, and if black can hit it, is there going to be a problem, but the odds are quite against this parlay. White must roll 6–2, 5–2, 4–2, 3–2, or 2–1, followed by black rolling any 2. This possibility gives 10/36 (the chances of rolling one

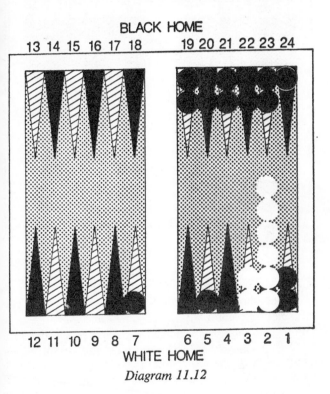

BLACK HOME

13 14 15 16 17 18   19 20 21 22 23 24

12 11 10 9 8 7   6 5 4 3 2 1

WHITE HOME

Diagram 11.12

of those bad numbers) times 11/36 (the chance of getting hit), which is in the neighborhood of 10 to 1 against.

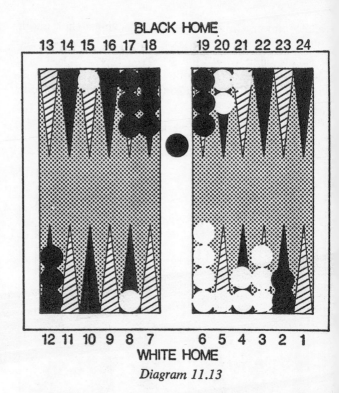

13 14 15 16 17 18   19 20 21 22 23 24

12 11 10 9 8 7   6 5 4 3 2 1

WHITE HOME

Diagram 11.13

Black should pass white's double. White can cover the blot on point 5 with 3's, 1's, 6–4 and 5–5—twenty-three combinations. Deduct one number for the fact that 3–3 is a terrible roll for white, and it still leaves white with 22/36 good rolls. Even if white doesn't roll one of these numbers, black may not roll well himself, giving white another chance.

210

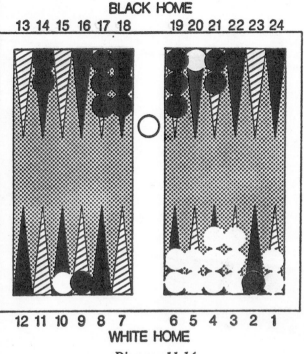

Diagram 11.14

White should not take black's double. Sixteen numbers will lead to point 20 (any number without a 4 or a 5). Furthermore, 4–1, 5–1, and 5–3 will hit the blot on point 10, giving black twenty-two good rolls.

White might consider taking the double in this position, but it would still be risky. The reason white can take this move, is because he has a chance to work the

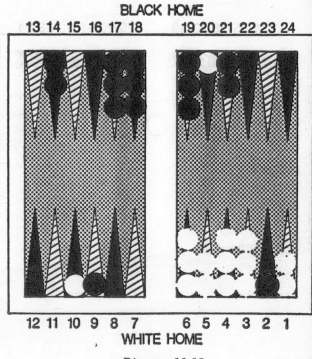

Diagram 11.15

black blot on point 2 into oblivion. Notice that white doesn't have a man on the bar as he did in Diagram 11.14. This situation means that even should black point on white at point 20, white can still come in and hit the blot on point 2—perhaps unlikely, but white can play for it if he wishes.

In 11–16 white should double though he is losing the race 55 to 45 in pips. If white hits black, black may lose a lot of time getting in and starting. Even if white

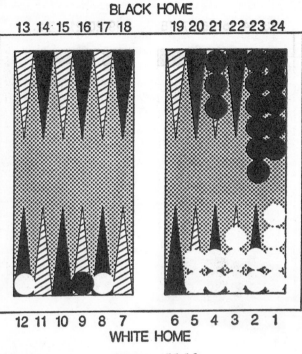

Diagram 11.16

misses, he will probably get some men off before black. Additionally, black will have misses right away if he rolls many 3's during his bear off.

However, black has a clear take. There won't be a gammon, and if black rolls well, he may be able to turn the cube back.

One way to look at a position like this is to consider it in terms of how many rolls one is ahead or behind, rather than thinking of pips.

Counting rolls is done when a player has arrived in an end position like this and is about to bear off. White may think, "I will have both my men in on this or the next roll. In any case, I can expect to have at least one man off at the end of two rolls. Black will be lucky to get a man off in two rolls, and even if he does, he may lose a roll if he misses with 3's, which will not take off a man for black. Therefore, I am at least one, and maybe more, rolls ahead of black if I *don't* hit him. If I do hit, I'll gain at least an extra roll, and perhaps even two, three, or more rolls if black fails to come in."

BLACK HOME

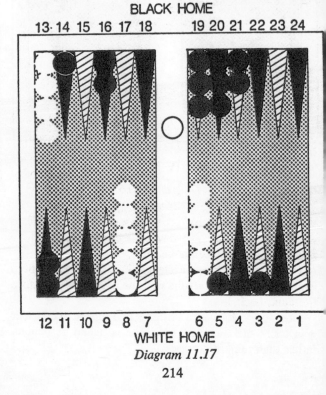

Diagram 11.17

In 11–17 black should double. White, if he comes in, will be very lucky if he doesn't leave a shot. 4–3, for instance, brings white's man on the bar onto point 22, but what does white do with the 4? The only safe way to play it is from point 6 to point 2, and this, as we have seen, is a waste of a man. White could conceivably get gammoned. White should pass.

BLACK HOME

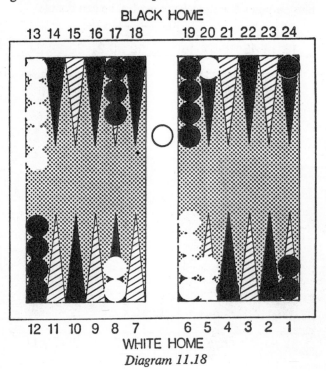

| 13 14 15 16 17 18 | 19 20 21 22 23 24 |

| 12 11 10 9 8 7 | 6 5 4 3 2 1 |

WHITE HOME

Diagram 11.18

White has a good position, but double would be premature. The favorable factors for white are his advantage in the race, black's poor position, which includes a blot on the 24 point, and the possibility of rolling 5's and 2's, which make the 20 point and the hit on the 4 point. White, incidently, does not want to hit the blot on the 24 point.

In black's favor is the fact that white's builders are piled up on the 6 point, and that if white rolls any 6 on this roll, it won't be good. If white, on roll, can hit the blot on point 4 and does not get hit, he can double.

BLACK HOME

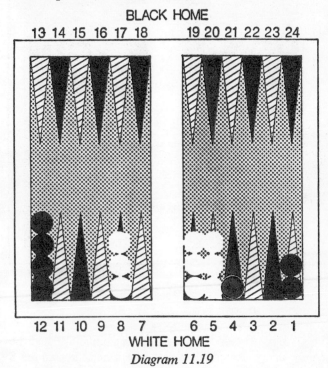

Diagram 11.19

Notice how the redistribution of white's men on his 8, 6, and 5 points gives him greater striking power than he had in Diagram 11.18. Here, white can hit from three points. Compare the distribution of white's men on those three points with that in Diagrams 11.18, 11.19, 11.20, and 11.21.

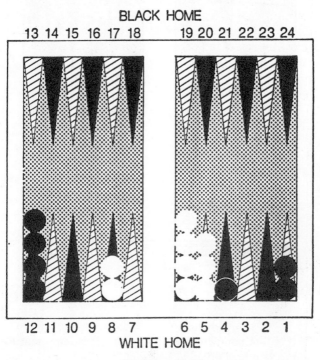

BLACK HOME
13 14 15 16 17 18   19 20 21 22 23 24

12 11 10 9 8 7   6 5 4 3 2 1
WHITE HOME

Diagram 11.20

White can still strike from three points, although he may have to leave an indirect shot if he hits from the 8 point.

In 11–21 white can effectively hit black from only

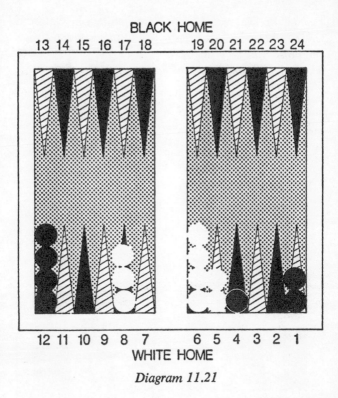

Diagram 11.21

two points, although in this instance he won't leave a blot on the point from which he hits. It is important to appreciate how different distributions of extra men can affect a position.

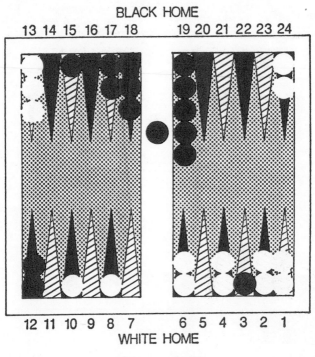

Diagram 11.22

Black should pass white's double. If black doesn't roll a 3, he can easily be gammoned. White will definitely, if possible, hit the black blot on point 5, should black come in there.

219

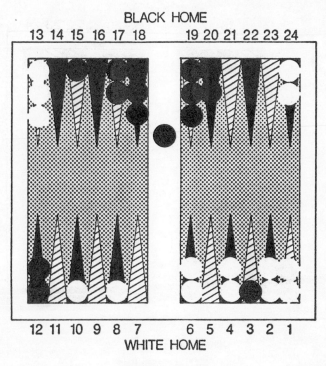

Diagram 11.23

This position is almost exactly like Diagram 11.22 but black's position is greatly strengthened by the 20 point. The difference of four points in a row is strong enough to take this double, which couldn't be taken in the previous position. In fact, white should probably not double yet. Close, but. . .

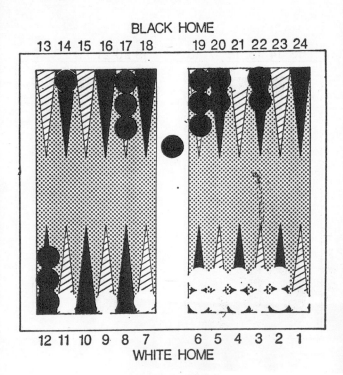

Diagram 11.24

White should play for the gammon. If white doesn't cover and black comes in, hitting the blot, white can still double and black would pass. If black's men were home, or near home, reducing white's chances for a gammon, white should double. Black should pass briskly if white doubles.

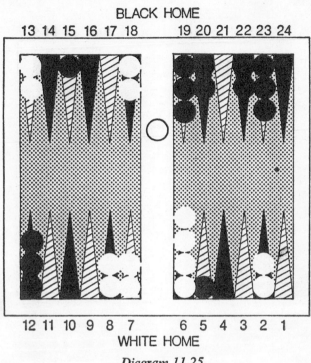

Diagram 11.25

Black's double should be passed. Even if white comes in, he won't be able to conduct a hitting war with black since that black board is too good. The black blot on point 15 is a threat to white if he comes in on point 21. White dare not hit that blot unless he rolls a 4–6. Certainly it would be disastrous for him to hit the blot on point 15 from point 18, which would leave two white blots where white can ill afford to leave them.

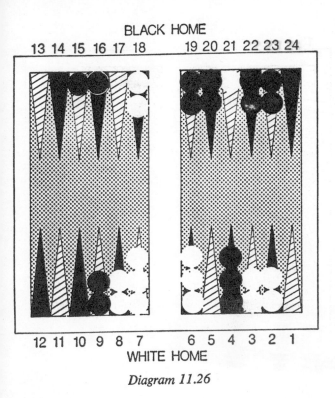

Diagram 11.26

Black should take a double. This position is just a bit early for a white double. If white rolls a 4 or a 1, he will hit only one man, unless he rolls 5–1, which hits two. However, 6–5, 5–2, and 6–3 hit only one checker also. White will be quite lucky to get his men safely home without leaving some shots. Only if white hits two men will he be likely to have time to get home without mishap.

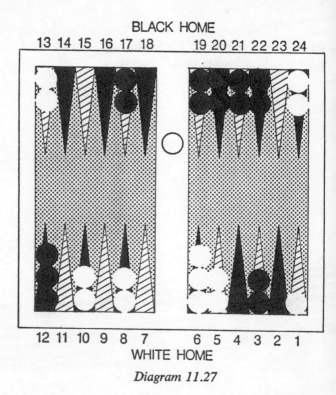

Diagram 11.27

White should pass a double quickly. Black's board is excellent and is likely to improve. Black will eventually bring some builders onto his board and onto his 17 point, and perhaps onto his outer board. White is in danger of being gammoned. Furthermore, white has a blot on his 1 point—a wasted man. It presents white with a Hobson's choice. Either white leaves the man there and risks its getting hit, should white be able to put a black man on the bar, or white can waste yet another man and cover it. White can't win unless he can form a prime in front of black, and any men on the 1 point will be valueless in this regard.

BLACK HOME

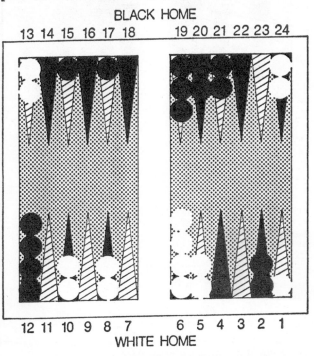

12 11 10 9 8 7   6 5 4 3 2 1
WHITE HOME

Diagram 11.28

White can take this double. This is the same as Diagram 11.27, but black's game has been weakened by removing two points. The overwhelming weakness in white's game is still that blot on his 1 point. Without that blot, white would happily accept this double, but even as it is, the take is acceptable.

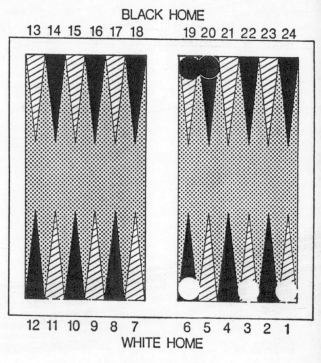

12 11 10 9 8 7   6 5 4 3 2 1
WHITE HOME

Diagram 11.29

White should double and black should resign. There is no number that won't take a man off for white, and only 2–1 and 4–1 leave white with a poor position. On the other hand, black should double if it is his roll, and white should pass.

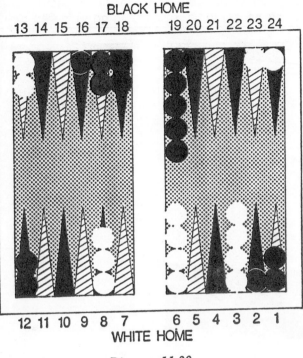

BLACK HOME

13 14 15 16 17 18   19 20 21 22 23 24

12 11 10 9 8 7   6 5 4 3 2 1

WHITE HOME

Diagram 11.30

Black has doubled and white quite properly has accepted. Black's double is a bit sporty to say the least. As a general guideline, one might resist the urge to double early in the game until he has made either the 5 or the 4 points. Black's builders are poorly located.

There is only one on point 16, and he has no extra men remaining on the 12 point.

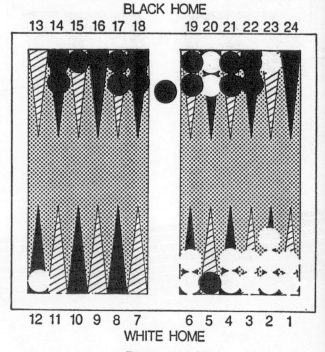

BLACK HOME

13 14 15 16 17 18   19 20 21 22 23 24

12 11 10 9 8 7   6 5 4 3 2 1

WHITE HOME

Diagram 11.31

White should double. He has a chance to pick up another prisoner if he rolls a 5 or 4–1 and could, with luck, get a gammon out of it. Black probably should pass because of the dangers of a gammon. It is possible for black to end up on the bar with three men looking at a closed board.

13 14 15 16 17 18   19 20 21 22 23 24

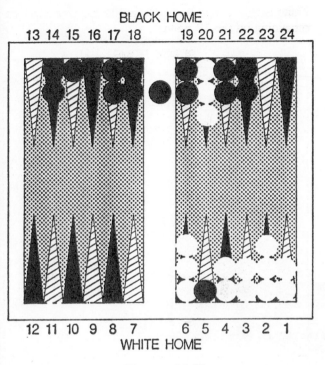

12 11 10 9 8 7   6 5 4 3 2 1

Diagram 11.32

Black should quickly give up. White hits with 5's and can also hit and run with 1–1, 1–2, 1–3, and 1–4. White's man which was on point 23 (see Diagram 11.31) has moved safely to point 20 and can escape safely with 4's. White can't play 6's, unless he also rolls a 4 or a 5, in which case there will be no problem. Only 3–3, 3–2, and 2–2 will be embarrassing for white.

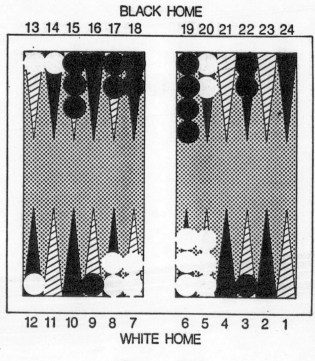

Diagram 11.33

White's double should be passed quite happily by black. White hits with 3's, 4's, 5's, and some combinations. Black is in significant danger of being gammoned and should give up the game.

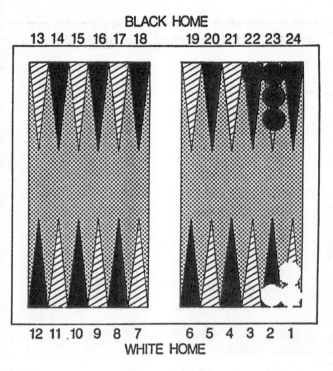

BLACK HOME

13 14 15 16 17 18   19 20 21 22 23 24

12 11 10 9 8 7   6 5 4 3 2 1

WHITE HOME

Diagram 11.34

Black has doubled and white has accepted. The double is bad. Even if black doesn't roll a 1, white can win by rolling doubles. If black does roll a 1, taking only one man off, white will redouble, and black will have to pass. Black, if he rolls a 1 on either this turn or (barring doubles) on his next turn, will lose.

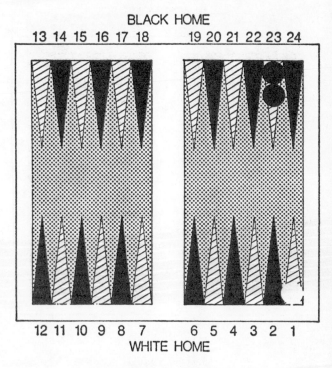

BLACK HOME

13 14 15 16 17 18   19 20 21 22 23 24

12 11 10 9 8 7   6 5 4 3 2 1

WHITE HOME

Diagram 11.35

Black should double and white should take. As discussed in the section on doubling, one should take if the odds against are 3–1 or less. Here the odds are 26/10. Twenty-six rolls win for black, and ten lose. The numbers that lose are any ace, except double aces.

The odds, therefore, are just under 3 to 1, and white should take.

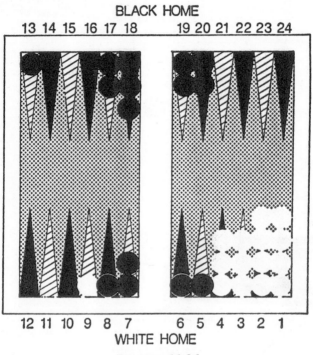

BLACK HOME

13 14 15 16 17 18   19 20 21 22 23 24

12 11 10 9 8 7   6 5 4 3 2 1

WHITE HOME

Diagram 11.36

White should not double. Black will be surely gammoned unless white rolls 3–1, 2–1, 1–1, or 2–2. Any other number gets white in and bearing off. White will be off in nine rolls, and possibly eight. Black is at least eleven, and probably twelve or thirteen rolls, away from averting a gammon.

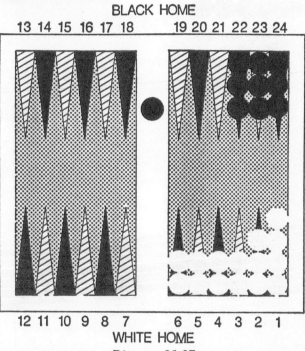

13 14 15 16 17 18   19 20 21 22 23 24

12 11 10 9 8 7   6 5 4 3 2 1

WHITE HOME

Diagram 11.37

Black has taken five men off before being hit and sent back. White, who has closed his board, doubles. Should black take?

This decision is quite close, but most players pass in black's position unless they have taken off six men or more. White will probably be off in eight or nine rolls, and black will have to come in almost immediately if he hopes to win.

BLACK HOME

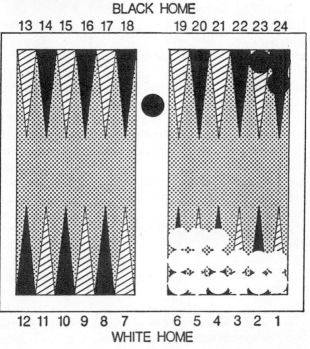

Diagram 11.38

In this position, black has managed to take eleven men off before being hit. Black is now on the bar, and white again has a closed board. This time, however, it is black who doubles. Should white accept? In this case, the answer is no. Again, it is a matter of rolls, and black expects to be in within three or four rolls and should be able to get that man around and his others off in seven or eight rolls. White is at least eight rolls away from getting off and will be lucky not to take ten or more.

Now if black had only ten men off, it would be a different story. That extra man for black will more often than not cost at least one roll. Black, with ten men off, should double, but this time white would take.

If black has taken seven, eight, or nine men off, neither player should contemplate a double until a few turns have passed.

In this position, 11–39, black is the favorite. But until a few moves have been consummated and white has or has not come in, no one can double. A position like this might arise when white has played for the gammon and has been hit at the last moment. In such a case, the cube might well still be in the middle. If white is lucky and comes in right away, he can double. Should white stay out for a few rolls, it will be black who doubles. In this position, a double by either player would be premature.

In Diagram 11.40, white doubles. Should black take? This is another case of counting the remaining rolls. White should be off in six rolls, or seven rolls if he is moderately unlucky. Black, on the other hand, is faced with an unclear number of rolls. Let's assume black comes in right away—against the odds, but we can give black this one slice of luck for the moment. Assuming he rolls average dice, black will be able to get that man around the board and home by his third roll. On this third roll, black will also, most likely, be able to take one man off

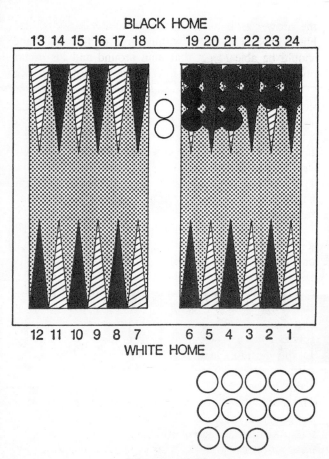

Diagram 11.39

from his board. If this is the case, black will then be able to get his men off in a total of six rolls, if he does not have a miss. White then has the following factors in his favor:

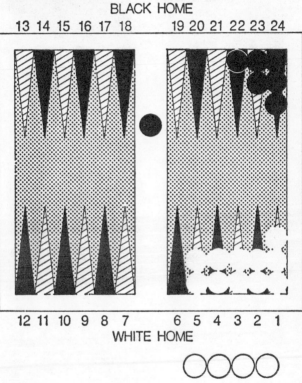

Diagram 11.40

1. Black may not come in at his first chance, thus costing him at least one roll.

2. It is white's roll in what is a six roll versus at best has a six-roll position.

3. Black may miss after he gets his man home.

All in all, black should pass this double.

In these positions, when computing rolls, one should assume an average roll to be about eight, taking doubles into consideration.

DO YOU KNOW HOW TO . . . ?
(Pinnacle Books can help you)

Be a full-fledged witch?
CAST YOUR OWN SPELL, Sybil Leek — P656 — 1.25

Select a sex therapist?
THE SEX DOCTORS!, Santini — P678 — 1.95

Benefit from meditation?
MEDITATION:
A Step Beyond with Edgar Cayce, Bakar — P547 — 1.25

Garden—dirt cheap!
THE FREE EARTH GUIDE TO
GARDENING, Kramer — P567 — 1.95

Get the most from your doctor's appointment?
HOW TO HELP YOUR DOCTOR HELP
YOU, Gaver — P587 — 1.75

Lose weight without counting calories?
THE THIN BOOK, By a Formerly Fat
Psychiatrist, Rubin, M.D. — P777 — 1.25

Stop those headaches!
WHAT YOU CAN DO ABOUT YOUR
HEADACHES, Hass, M.D. & Dolan — P301 — .95

Improve your lifestyle?
RECYCLE YOUR LIFESTYLE,
(The "Psychoenergetics Way"), Mok, M.D. — P118 — .95

Use your mind to improve your health?
PSYCHOSOMATICS, (How Your Emotions
Can Damage Your Health) H & M Lewis — P532 — 1.75

Become a complete person?
BODYMIND, (The Whole Person Health
Book) Miller — P566 — 1.50

YOU CAN ORDER ANY OF THESE BOOKS RIGHT HERE:
Please add 25¢ per book for postage and handling up to $1.00—
free thereafter.

Pinnacle Books
275 Madison Avenue
New York, N.Y. 10016

Please send me:

____P656 ____P678 ____P547 ____P567 ____P587

____P077 ____P301 ____P118 ____P532 ____P566

____Check here if you wish to receive our free catalog

PB-24

DO YOU KNOW HOW TO?
(Pinnacle does and can help you!)

CHECK WHICH TITLES HAVE THE MOST APPEAL FOR YOU!

3 PINNACLE COOKBOOKS WITH GREAT POPULAR ACCLAIM

_____THE NEW COOK'S COOKBOOK
by Carol Guilford   P042 $1.25

_____THE U.S. GOVERNMENT BUDGET COOK-
BOOK by Karen Dent   P031 $1.25

_____THE LOW CARBOHYDRATE DIET COOK-
BOOK by William Thorne   P261 $1.25

3 DIET BOOKS FROM PINNACLE THAT HAVE HELPED THOUSANDS

The top bestseller!
_____THE THIN BOOK, By a Formerly Fat Psychiatrist
by Theodore Isaac Rubin, M.D.   P777 $1.25

_____THE DIET BOOK: All About Diets—The Best
One for You by Carol Guilford   P239 $1.25

_____THE 100-CALORIE MIRACLE DIET by world
famous model and photographer, Bunny Yeager
P519 $1.50

3 BOOKS THAT CAN CHANGE YOUR LIFE STYLE

_____RECYCLE YOUR LIFESTYLE: The "Psycho-
energetics" Way, by Dr. Paul Mok   P118   95¢

_____EXECUTIVE YOGA: A Practical System of
Health and Exercise for the Busy Man by Harvey
Day   P098 $1.25

_____WHAT YOU CAN DO ABOUT YOUR HEAD-
ACHES by Frederick J. Hass, M.D. & Edward F.
Dolan, Jr.   P301   95¢

Take this check list to your local paperback store. If you cannot find any of these books, simply send the cover price plus 25¢ each for postage and handling to:
PINNACLE BOOKS,
275 Madison Avenue, New York, N.Y. 10016